TENDRING PENINSULA

LAND OF MILK AND HUNNYE

3 old cottages in Lower Street, Kirby-le-Soken. Now the Ship Inn carpark. In the foreground Mr Alf Whipps. c.1910

TENDRING PENINSULA

LAND OF MILK AND HUNNYE

Peter Ford

IAN HENRY PUBLICATIONS

The map on the cover is
Army map of 1805, railway added in 1882

British Library Cataloguing in Publication Data

Ford, Peter C.
Tendring Hundred : land of milk and
hunnye.
1. Essex. (District) Tendring. Trade,
history
1. Title
380.1'09426'725

ISBN 0-86025-420-8

Printed by
Booksprint, 1a Marsh Lane, Ashton, Bristol, BS3 2NR
for
Ian Henry Publications, Ltd.
20 Park Drive, Romford, Essex RM1 4LH

PREFACE

If, like me, you are prone to lean over bridges and sea walls soaking up unspoilt views with open mind, allowing events of the past to float like welcome ghosts through your thoughts, and if you imagine the plod of a hoof and ring of anvil may still be there in the modern brash roaring symphony of traffic – then this offering of bits and pieces from years gone by, inspired by the tranquil peace of Kirby Quay, might, I hope, help you to continue gazing nostalgically at our heritage in reflective enjoyment.

Peter C Ford
Frinton, 1988

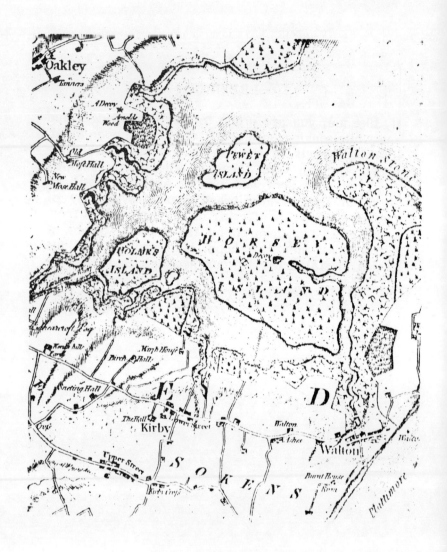

Chapman & André map. 1777

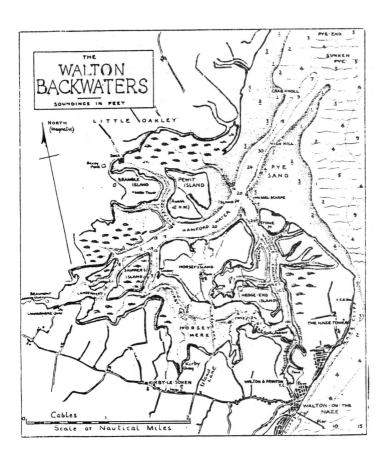

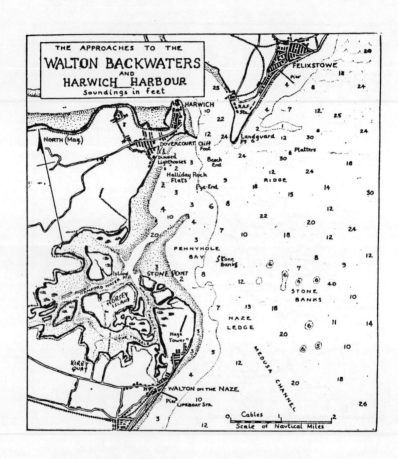

THE APPROACHES TO THE

WALTON BACKWATERS
AND
HARWICH HARBOUR
Soundings in feet

FELIXSTOWE

NORTH (Mag.)

HARWICH

DOVERCOURT Cliff Foot

disused Lighthouses

Halliday Rock Flats

Pye-End

Beach End

Landguard Pt

Platters

RIDGE

PENNYHOLE BAY

Stone Banks

STONE POINT

ISLAND PT

STANFORD WATER

HORSEY ISLAND

NAZE LEDGE

STONE BANKS

MEDUSA CHANNEL

Naze Tower

THE TWIZZLE

KIRBY QUAY

WALTON on the NAZE

Pier LIFEBOAT STA.

Cables

Scale of Nautical Miles

Chapter One

The mid-18th century topographer, John Norden, visiting north east Essex observed it was 'most fatte, fruteful and full of profitable thinges, exceeding (as far as I can find) anie other shire for the general commodities and the plenty... This shire seemeth to me to deserve the title of the Englishe Goshen, the fattest of the lande, comparable to Palestrina, that flowed with milk and hunnye'.

When in Tendring Hundred he admired the local cheeses 'great and huge, and wondered at for their massiveness'. Alas, the cheeses are no more, but this Goshen, a place of light and plenty, still enjoys July sunshine averages of over seven hours a day. Local honey can still be purchased and some of the fields support herds of Frisian cows, a Dutch breed it is true, but now so familiar that we regard them as our own.

Making due allowance for 18th century exuberance of language it can still be agreed that the salt water edged 'Goshen' of Tendring Hundred, gently encroached by Hamford (sometimes called Hainford, Handford, and earlier still Hand or Hand-fleet) Water is a lovely and historic place.

It is not clear where the boundaries of John

1

Norden's 'Goshen' were, but they must have included the area between Harwich, Manningtree, Clacton and Walton, a matter of some 200 square miles with no more than a 16 mile journey between main towns. While this book shines the spotlight of history on this locality, a general picture of conditions in England, at least in East Anglia, is discovered, as many ancient customs are common to all, especially in the coastal regions.

Before the advent of railways last century, when roads were gravel at best and mire at worst, small muddy Essex creeks were life-lines, especially to the Sokens. Rarely would Hamford Water be without masts and sails of barges, sloops and smacks shewing above reeds and banks of the waterways.

Kirby Quay to the north of Kirby-le-Soken and south of the Hamford Water is today a quiet, peaceful backwater, frequented by occasional private yachtsmen, birdwatchers or ramblers. The creaking of rigging and spars is now a century-old memory. However, abundant bird life remains, as of old, probing in and feeding on mudflats and saltings. Brent geese in adjacent fields maintain constant conversation, backed by the wild cries of sanderling, godwit, curlew, tern, dunlin, turnstone, grey plover, ringed plover, oyster catcher, gull and many species of duck, feeding in relative peace from wildfowlers.

If, as some experts suggest, there is such a thing as inherited memory, they will be grateful that the 30 foot steam launch *Tyche*, used by Colonel Davis of New House Farm in the 1890s is no longer around for wildfowling, with its cunningly designed hinged funnel and low gunwhales, ideal for hiding in the shelter of the Twizzle, between Horsey Island and Kirby Quay. With its two swivelling fowling guns mounted forward, one of them a two inch breech loader and the other a one and a quarter inch muzzle loader, firing power was formidable. Brent, teal and

2

Entrance to Hamford Water as seen from Dovercourt. Walton on horizon. Appearing welcoming, this wide stretch of water is treacherous, shallow, roack and shoal ridden!

High tide flooding over causeway from Kirby Creek to Pilot's Pool

3

widgeon were shot in their hundreds – and so was anything else that moved. In addition many birds were taken by locals and eaten or sold in the Sokens, sometimes even in Colchester, transported by carrier on Monday, Wednesday or Saturday.

The rich feeding grounds of Hamford Water were exploited to the full centuries ago and the Chapman & André map of 1777 shews a decoy pond on Horsey Island and another to the north of Old Mose (now Moze) Hall, Beaumont. Many a local family relied on legal or illegal meat from the backwaters, be it partridge, rabbit, hare, wildfowl or flatfish, the latter scraped from the mud by hand at low tide – outlines of the fish being clearly visible below the mud and easily scooped into a bucket. For many generations, until the 17th century, there were extensive oyster beds in Hamford Water; now there are very few in the Walton backwaters.

The main activity around Kirby Creek was, however, shipping and, when it is remembered there were no auxiliary engines, the skill of the sailing barge skippers appears masterly, faced as they were with narrow shallow creeks, requiring elaborate tacking with only wind and judgment to avoid grounding on mud or gravel. Although navigable parts of the creeks were marked by withies it needed considerable knowledge and seamanship to interpret the marks to navigate such tortuous channels in safety. No wonder there was a pilot's cottage to the west of Pilot's Pool, south of Kirby Quay (still standing, as a modernised house, today).

Hufflers would watch the tides and, seeing masts and sails approaching from Hamford Water, would appear above the rushes as if by magic to pull or help turn the barges when the weather was still or adverse. Research has not yet revealed how much they were paid, but it has been suggested that contraband or barter was sometimes involved. Some hufflers also provisioned ships as freelance chandlers. In Heligoland they were both pilots and ship victuallers. The term was also used for vessels.

The Kirby 1851 Census lists one licensed victualler, but in White's 1848 *Directory* there are three - Thos Hammond of the Hare & Hounds; George Lee, Master Mariner, of the Red Lion; and James Haywood of the Ship. Being so conveniently placed for the quay, they must have acted as ships' chandlers, supplying at least food and drink and probably much else.

Chandlers, whatever their speciality, were only too happy to supply other goods not normally stocked. For instance, in Gravesend even today, leading shipping butchers will, if requested, supply ships with tackle and clothing they obtain from other chandlers specialising therein. And, of course, vice versa. Mercantile Marine outfitters in the town also supply ships' chandlers with clothing and uniforms. They all give each other friendly discounts of 10% on items supplied, enabling the chandler with the actual shipping order to invoice the total to the ship on one bill: an age old custom, saving office work and of much benefit to old time barge masters who had little time or inclination for paper work.

Kirby Quay is narrow even at high tide and manually turning any craft is difficult; nevertheless, skippers preferred to moor stern first ready for departure when laden as soon as a southerly wind blew and, if possible, without the expense of assistance. This type of mooring could be important in saving time and money. Depending on wind or weather, vessels might have to be towed in by the crew of mate and boy cook rowing in the dinghy or they could even winch in, using a kedge anchor carried, rowed or thrown ashore to lodge in bank or mud, enabling an attached line coupled to the hand operated winch to wind her in. Either way, craft had to be turned round by lugging on ropes when at the quay, ready for departure.

With urgent cargoes or if facing fierce competition from others, barges were also often towed out of creeks by the crew in a dinghy in minimum water to areas offering enough sea room to use the sails.

Until late in the 19th century steam tugs were not available, but even then, they would be virtually impossible to use in the narrow confines of Hamford Water. This is confirmed by a correspondent signing himself 'Antelope' in a letter to the Editor of the *Walton & Clacton Gazette* on 12 September, 1886, referring to the helpfulness of Mr David Lay, the pilot, in placing pots, pans, barrels and old baskets on sticks to mark the safe channels. He then concludes with obvious old timer's relish, 'I once saw a Government steam tug in Handford Water stuck three times in mud'.

We can speculate on how many free pints of beer accompanied the recounting of this in the local inns!

Considerable concentration is needed even today when entering the Creek in an auxiliary powered craft. Walton Backwaters are not unlike a small--scale Norfolk Broad, fortunately providing protection in almost any weather, but tricky. The entrance is half a mile off Dovercourt foreshore, south of the mouth of Harwich Harbour. Stone Banks buoy marks isolated clumps of rock and stone covered by only a fathom of water at low tide. Pye-End buoy marks the northern extremity of a long tongue of hard sand, known as Pye Sand and the Sunken Pye. The shallowest part of the approach is Halliday Rock Flats with less than a fathom of water in places at low tide. Sailing barges preferred to wait until two or three hours of flood tide before attempting entrance to the Backwaters.

In a northeast gale at night it could be decidedly

Deceptively wide appearance of seaway at ¾ tide

Kirby Creek was marked with withies at low tide

hazardous. The Channel from Crab Knoll to High Hill narrows to a bottleneck of little more than a cable in width, widening into Hamford Water, with about three cables of water varying between four and five fathoms.

From Hamford Water, Kirby Creek in a southerly direction has a depth of one fathom for half a mile. Completely protected anchorage was available between Skippers and Horsey Islands should berths be full. Elderly locals remember talk of 5 barges at a time waiting for berths on several occasions. Kirby Creek then turns sharply east into the shallows of Horsey Mere and, finally, south again to Kirby Quay. The tortuous gutway, marked with withies, needed as much skill to navigate as skiers tackling marker flags on steep ski runs this century.

At high tide, navigable waters appear extensive to the uninitiated viewing from sea walls, but mud and sand bank hazards and narrow twisting channels are daunting when exposed and viewed at low tide. Admiration for the doughty and skilled barge skippers of old grows apace at the brilliant seamanship involved.

No mechanical diggers kept channels clear, as they do today off Harwich and Felixstowe. Occasionally, local fishing smacks would perform incidental dredging in their search for cement stone, copperas, oysters, oyster spat and mussels. As only three small streams feed Hamford Water and no rivers scour the bottom when in flood after a thaw or rainstorm and, as the tide flows at only about $2\frac{1}{2}$ knots, there is little natural help with dredging.

The passage of the sailing barges themselves did, in fact, act as a scouring agent and the Kirby Quay area was also kept clear of silt by opening the sluice gates separating Pilot's Pool from the wharf at low tide. This is done even today by the owners of Quay House (the old granary) and Quay.

With little outflow pollution, except from the late 20th century curse of leached chemical pesticides, herbicides and artificial fertilisers, Hamford Water is one of our cleanest sheltered inlets. Ideal for oysters, as can be seen in another chapter.

Before considering the type of cargo loaded and unloaded at Kirby Quay in the days of sail, it can be noted that in 1326 whale meat may have arrived at the berth from Walton, where an 80 foot whale was beached on 19th January. The tongue was reserved for the Bishop of London, the rest being carried away by 32 named men from Little Holland, Kirby, Frinton, Tendring, Arewell, Harwich, Mose, Beaumont, St Osyth and Waltham [Walton?]. Even with 32 men sharing the whale each portion would be heavy, messy, bloody and smelly, apart from being unwieldy and flabby. With roads as they were, a boat would be the easiest way for delivering such welcome gifts of fresh winter meat to Kirby people. We shall never know how it arrived nor will we know whether the tongue was still fresh when eventually it arrived in London at the Bishop's Palace, after at least two days by horse delivery!

Until the late 19th century cargo from the sailing barges at Kirby Quay was just about everything heavy and bulky needed by the local community; sand and gravel from Frinton and Great Holland, chalk from Gravesend and Purfleet to make into lime or marl as fertilisers, occasionally Kentish ragstone for specific building and sea walls, bricks, coal from north east coal mines, manure from London, perhaps Baltic and continental wheat as at Mistley and, of course, locally caught fish. Fishing smacks, when dredging for oysters, also hauled in copperas (a bisulphide of iron used to make green vitriol for dyeing and for ink) to be delivered to the Walton Copperas Works - until about 1880 - and septaria, the local cement stone, for the several cement works at Harwich. Having unloaded the local requirements, the heavier items, such as copperas and septaria, were left on board for delivery to Walton and Harwich via the water.

Refreshment for the crews could be had at the Royal Oak (now gone), the Lion (now Red Lion), and the Ship. If the Customs Man was not in sight ashore and if the Revenue Cutter (an unpopular posting in view of the alleged unhealthiness of the ague probably malaria - in those times) had not been alerted, contraband could be disposed of discreetly, as the area had been renowned for smuggling for generations. As recently as 1913 the King's Head at Landermere (now gone) is reputed to have lost its licence for just that!

In this wild and remote region, off the main roads, a quiet midnight walk along the sea wall from Island Lane to Kirby Quay, with only the eerie cries of oyster-catchers probing mud to find cockles by touch, will, even today, allow imaginations to re-create the muffled curses and instructions from sailing barge crews to contacts ashore about barrels and bottles of spirits and wine not intended for Customs and Excise attention. With luck and perseverance it might even be possible to hear the donkeys once stabled at Kirby Quay stamping hooves in readiness for clandestine night deliveries.

For many years the local Customs Man lived in Lower Street, Kirby, and in 1850 was collecting £5 per annum light dues from vessels in Hamford Water. By 1868 he had been transferred to Walton - one might well wonder why! At this time the population of Kirby was over 900, while that of Walton was only 500. Possibly he was moved because beach, rather than creek, smuggling had increased or, and this is only speculation, because communities were small and everybody knew each other, so smuggling must have been obvious to all including the Customs Man, who may well have turned a diplomatic blind eye for the sake of peace and harmony. The authorities, with this suspicion in mind, may have deemed it better to have him moved to Walton. If this supposition is unfounded, apologies to his memory – but moved he definitely was.

Kirby-le-Soken was well organised and ideally situated for smuggling and had been for centuries. Inevitably, as with most villages sited near the open sea, it is alleged that a smugglers' tunnel existed between the Lion and the saltings in Horsey Mere also used, it is said, by Huguenot refugees. A slightly unusual feature to this legend is that it is reputed that the tunnel was only bricked up by the brewers in 1946 because of its dangerous condition. However, despite exhaustive enquiries to brewers, local builders and retired staff, so far no one has been found who actually saw the tunnel. The most convincing wet blanket on this story is that there are no cellars in the Red Lion, no brick drains leading to the creek which could be elevated and glamourised into the status of smugglers' tunnel, and, above all, no visual evidence of any comparitively recent brickwork.

In any case, the inn is only a few feet above high tide level and any tunnel below ground would flood with monotonous and inconvenient frequency. This romantic story can therefore only be used to support the incontrovertible fact that villages around Hamford Water were smuggling-orientated and therefore subject to the usual fictional accretions of dramatic legends.

For those reluctant to dismiss this intriguing story, there is another ancient road (now only a footpath) leading to the saltings and it was once almost a tunnel between banks and elm trees, dipping gently into a dyke flowing near Kirby Creek. Unfortunately for the romance of the story it is nearer the Ship Inn than the Red Lion!

For a gripping and historically accurate account of smuggling activities in this area, Hervey Benham in his *The Smugglers' Century* gives a full account. It is certain that much highly organised and profitable smuggling took place in and around Kirby, indicating illicit trade far more extensive than the occasional packet of tobacco or bottle of spirits.

Exports from Kirby Quay were mainly produce from local farms in the shape of hay and straw for the thousands of horses in London (to be re-cycled into manure for import in due course), a considerable amount of wheat and barley, bricks from several small brickfields and even lime from the limekiln at Kirby Quay.

A retired barge skipper was questioned shortly after the last war by a local resident about the problems of shipping grain in barges newly emptied of London manure and he asserted that there was no problem as the holds were scrubbed out before loading. There were no hoses, only buckets of creek water. Bilge pumps were hand operated, so high pressure hosing was impossible and drying time limited. One wonders about the alleged extra flavour of old fashioned bread!

Exporting cereals, straw and hay from the Sokens is centuries old as the area has been recognised since time immemorial as a corn growing region of considerable merit. Much of the Tendring Hundred was never subject to the hated Forest Laws reserving hunting rights to the Crown, so was without many restrictions on agriculture. Since before Roman times the fertile soil was cultivated and on the islands sheep grazed.

Many Roman buildings survived for generations without occupants. Gradually stones, bricks and tiles were filched from the sites to be used in new building. Many churches, especially in Essex, shew in their walls remnants of this salvage used in this stone-bereft county as fillings for walls. Often the comment is made that Roman cement is long lasting (which it is), but this can be misleading as the term 'Roman cement' refers to the unique cement made in east Essex from cement stone or septaria.

'Roman cement' was patented by James Parker of Northfleet in 1796 and is sometimes called 'Parker's Cement' or, as he preferred, 'Aquatic Cement'. It was much stronger and harder than other cements and would even set under water, thus also being known as 'Hydraulic cement'. Because of these properties it was useful for stopping broken water pipes and for preventing inflows of water. Another use was as stucco, facing bricks on buildings. As this stone occurs in London clay, the cliffs at Walton on the Naze, being continually lashed by the sea, are a rich and easy source, as dredgermen last century knew only too well from the contents of their nets. Instead of retrieving the stone as building material, as did the Romans, they sailed to Harwich and sold the cargo to any one of the five cement works active in 1832 or to one of the three larger factories in 1851, for manufacture into cement.

This was a major local industry. The stone was broken into small chippings, then burnt in kilns just as chalk is turned into lime. The resulting product was packed into casks of about 4 cwt each and sold in London in 1852, for instance, at seven shillings and sixpence a cask. Two million bushels of this cement were produced annually at Harwich, yielding 30 to 40 shillings a ton. Rather than wait to dredge after storms or high tides, so much digging of the cliffs went on that erosion soon became a problem. Beacon Cliff at Harwich receded to such an extent that the actual strength of the tides was changed and the silting up of Harwich Harbour threatened. The Commission on Harbours of Refuge

Horsey Island from Peter's Point. Any breach in the sea wall of such a low lying island is serious.

Sewage outfall at Harwich in Roman cement

recommended in 1845 that removal of septaria stone should be stopped and a stone breakwater be built to restore former direction and force of the tides: this was done and it still exists.

Dredging thus became the only way to obtain this valuable cement stone, much to the benefit of local dredgermen. In 1845 smacks with three or four crew numbered two to three hundred, each racing (cutter rigged) to favourite dredging grounds. Many boats came from Kent and some from Harwich and Hamford Water. West Rocks, off Walton, where currents had accumulated vast heaps, was regarded as the best place.

The industry began to decline in the 1870s as cement stone was supplanted by Kentish Portland Cement made from readily available chalk quarries in Rosherville, Swanscombe and Northfleet, depletion of which has removed complete hills of chalk, some finding its way as lime fertiliser to farms around Hamford Water via barges at Kirby, Beaumont and Landermere Quays until the 1920s.

Artefacts held together with the original 'Roman' cement still remain in the area and, as one labourer who worked on the Harwich sewage outfall a few years ago said, "The ruddy cement was harder than the stone!"

Chapter Two

*Red Hills - Salt pans - Flooding - Weather - Corn prices
- Huguenots - The Harriet - Census - Maps - Skipper
family - Clocks*

After the Romans, the Saxons and Danes (who gave
names to many villages and hamlets) also saw the
merits of the area for agriculture. In support of this,
Canon J Allen in his unpublished *History of the
Parish of Beaumont,* c. 1960, states that one
chronicler said Beaumont history began with the
coming of the Romans (not verified and, in any case,
Beaker People remains have been found there) and
that the road running from Beaumont Quay was
originally Roman, leading to Colchester. He also
reported that Miller Christy said the Roman road
from Colchester to the west via Bishop's Stortford
began at Beaumont Quay, going almost due west
along the parish boundary between Beaumont and
Thorpe-le-Soken for nearly two miles to a point on
Holland Brook near Hannams Hall, Tendring. There-
after the road is said to run into Tendring as far as
the church and then all trace is lost.

We do know that the Romans had access from
the coast to St Albans, Braintree, Halstead and
Cambridge. In Gosfield and Halstead there were
villas which would have been connected by more
than tracks, so possibly oysters, corn, timber,
pottery and wine would progress through Tendring

16

Hundred in ox drawn wagons. Further research using aerial photography and selected digging will throw more light on the subject.

Hamford Water was well known for salt pans: as far back as the Domesday Book two were listed at Great Oakley, three at Moze and two at Beaumont. Salt pans at Beaumont-cum-Moze were only destroyed recently. Apart from general cooking and preserving, salt was essential for marsh-made cheese. Salt pans were shallow ponds allowing sea water in and capable of being shut off so that salt water could be evaporated, leaving salt crystals to be scraped off when dry: a valuable asset to the Romans and to succeeding generations. The process could be accelerated by using bonfires under crocks to assist evaporation and circles of fire reddened earth (known as Red Hills) remain to this day.

The Victoria History of Essex lists five Red Hills within the seawall near Beaumont Hall and the Church and others south of Skippers Island. A Roman coin was found in 1929 and also pottery, hand-made sherds and a red deer antler. More sherds were found over a wide area outside the present seawall at Kirby Quay, presumed to be from a rubbish dump on the edge of a Red Hill eroded by the tide about a hundred yards north east of Quay House and about 20 feet east of the seawall.

Red Hills are low mounds two to five feet in height of variable shape from half to thirty acres in size. The body of the mound is almost entirely burnt earth of bright red colour and full of variously shaped pieces of soft, coarse burnt clay containing marks of straw or grass. These fragments, known as briquetage, came from large vessels or tanks with sides $\frac{3}{4}$ inch thick and also from broken fire-bars. Some hills shew signs of domestic pottery, both Iron Age and Belgic: most, however, is Roman, although some have been dated 4th century. It is thought these extensive sites were not used as potters' works as no kilns have been found.

Direct evidence upon the purpose of the Red Hills is lacking, but it seems certain they were connected with salt making. They are always sited on the coast, usually on saltings outside the seawalls (if inside, this is because the wall has been built subsequently) and above average high tide level, becoming islands at spring tide.

The red earth is probably the remains of peat or turf used as fuel over a very long period. Where the London clay meets the sea, as in north east Essex and, particularly, Hamford with its quiet waters, the necessary pans and crude fireplaces could be made from that clay on site. With the abundant brushwood locally available in those days and with turf to slow the rate of burning, these fires could burn for days under the evaporation pans.

No doubt for most people things remained much the same throughout the Dark and Middle Ages. Main disruptions to a settled life of seed-time and harvest, commerce and industry, came from unseasonable or extreme weather, floods and gales, rather than from the rarer political pressures. The sea in the 14th century was referred to as that 'unmerciful enemy the sea', and over three hundred years later, in 1798, the original Walton Parish Church was claimed by the same enemy, as indeed has much of the early town.

As far back as November, 1099, on the first day of the new moon (the feast of St Martin) it was reported that 'sea flood rose to such a height and did so much harm as no man remembered that it ever did before'. This was, of course, the old-time comment whenever high tides, driven by north east gales, occurred. It was always higher than in living memory! Again in 1236 on 12 November (St Martin's again) it was recorded that 'the most violent wind and damaging of sea and river' resulted in 'drowning of marshland'. This damage extended round the coast to Woolwich Marshes. There was another in 1251 and again in 1294, when a Royal Commission for Kent ordered banks to be raised at least four feet and widened in proportion to the extra height. A daunting and enormous task without earthmoving machinery.

No wonder that a Law of the Marsh had come into being. The principle was established that upkeep of sea defences was to be paid for a carried out by the beneficiaries in proportion to their lands and rights. Local responsibility, in other words, but with oversight by Royal Commissioners. This was in force until 1930 when the Land Drainage Act created government agencies to do the work.

Severe storm floods occurred in 1327, 1376 and 1382. By 1427 the King handed over the Commissioner's responsibilities to Parliament. The body responsible had the evocative title of Commissioners of Sewers, absorbing responsibility of oversight for walls, ditches, land drainage and sea encroachment. In 1515 by Act of Parliament, the 1427 Act was perpetuated.

More damage by excessively high tides took place in 1551 and 1555 and by storm in 1570. The cost of the last at Harwich was £14.18.7d, but much of the coastline as far as Dover was also devastated.

Courts of the Sewers were formed to watch local levels and the Tendring body was particularly concerned with the level of Frinton and Little Holland which was criticial. For many years, this remained the weak link on the coastline.

As time progressed, Commissioners became rare and the defence of the marshland depended more and more on the initiative, effort and means of responsible owners or tenants in the Approaches. An interesting document exists, signed on 25

September, 1691, concerning a breach in the back-waters which, because of drought in late summer and heavy thunderstorms on 20 August and 13 September, caused 'great loss of life at sea'.

Sir Harry Cambell of Birch Hall agreed with Richard French of Kirby, carpenter, and Thomas Hersham, labourer, that he would pay £30 of good and lawful money of England if they repaired a certain breach in the sea wall of Horsey Island: £15 to be paid when the breach was stopped and £15 when work was finished. Sir Harry to provide timber, broom, boats and boards. For fair play, independent assessors were appointed, Mr Thos Wood, Mr John Hacher and Mr Wm Spooner, in order to judge the well doing of the same.

Part payment or progress payments, as we would say today, were undoubtedly wise precautions as skullduggery and skimping were well recognised and practised. In the Great Flood of 1703, for instance, much damage in the Thames at Dagenham was caused through shoddy work and Parliament had to vote funds for the work in 1714: this took six years to complete. 'Fiddling' may be a modern euphemism, but the practice is ancient.

Another disastrous tide happened in 1736 and a damaging storm in 1791. As if this wasn't enough, Essex roads to the coast were reported as being impassable because of deep snow. A high peak in the poor rate of 1800 might have been as a result of that hard weather.

Worse was to come in 1816, a 'year without a summer', caused by the effects of the recent volcanic eruption in Sumbawa, east of Java, from the 9,255 feet high Mount Tamboro, recorded as a year with a temperature drop overall of 1° Fahrenheit and little sunshine, resulting in widespread crop failure. J M Stratton in *Agricultural Records (A.D. 220-1977)* mentions 1816 as a 'wet summer with very poor harvest. A winter of storm, gales and floods... snow lying on the ground in mid-April. July and August temperatures 4.8° below average... in the Midlands and North much corn was still in the fields in November... one of the most disastrous harvests known'.

Apparently wheat prices fluctuated violently and in 1816 were 78s.6d a quarter. They had been as high as 126s.6d in 1812, the highest recorded during the Napoleonic Wars, but had dropped to between 40 and 56 shillings from 1864 to 1871. Truly, farmers never knew how they were going to fare from year to year. The war with the United States from 1812 to 1815 caused a great disturbance to trade with abrupt fluctuations of demand and employment.

Nearer home, competitively priced European corn was shut off and this steadying influence on corn price was no more. The poor suffered terribly from the price of bread, especially when land cultivation was increased to take advantage of high prices. To make matters worse, after the Battle of Waterloo and the end of the Napoleonic Wars, the price of corn plummeted with the return of peace, many farmers being ruined and rents not paid. Prices tumbled yet further as many farmers gave up their leases in desperation. Agricultural depression began.

In 1815 the protective Corn Law was passed with the aim of restoring agricultural prosperity. Unfortunately this was at the expense of the consumer and there was violent opposition until the repeal of the Corn Laws in 1846.

So, although previous centuries can be imagined as tranquil years with little change and a steady flow of barges into Kirby Quay year after year with a consistent supply of the same types of produce, this is far from the truth.

Nature and, occasionally, politics and wars, have

always had their influence on continuity. Inevitably there have been peaks and valleys and even the relatively settled area of Tendring was not exempt.

A further interesting light on changing fortunes is seen from a report from religious refugees in the 17th century. After the revocation of the Edict of Nantes in 1685, a flood of Huguenot refugees came to England, many to the Sokens. Several were already there, but the newcomers, when asking for permission to build a place of worship and joining with compatriots, said, 'We live in a district not one of the least fertile in the Kingdom, but one which emigration to America or other causes has rendered almost desert, the country being less thickly inhabited than it might be, and considerable farms being uncultivated... now but a wilderness, overgrown with bracken and broom'. A graphic, yet sad, description of north east Essex.

With modern intensive farming, little bracken and broom remains in the Kirby area today, but it must once have been prolific for Sir Harry Cambell to agree to provide it for repairing Horsey Island breach in 1691.

Huguenot influence can still be seen in the several mansard roofed cottages in the Sokens. Could they but see them, their hearts might be warmed, but what they might think of the present vast hedge-less fields is probably best left unsaid.

Focussing again on Kirby Quay it can be assumed that by the 19th century the sailing barge traffic was relatively regular and settled, but memories of other dangers facing mariners in the century must have lingered long. The East Coast and English Channel were dangerous places for friend or foe: armed privateers from both sides of the Channel were active and Master and crew could well be taken and incarcerated on the continent, with their ship confiscated as a prize of war. Sometimes their craft was ransomed and generally Master and crew would be returned home after about a month, resolving, no doubt, to meet the enemy on an equal or advantageous position in future - the enemy being usually the French.

A glimmer of light on the actual state of affairs faced by east coast mariners in those days can be gathered from reading (and also between the lines) the Bill of Sale of the vessel *The Harriett,* signed and sealed on 23 April, 1816, in Kirby-le-Soken. It is worthy of detailed quoting as a salty tang of the sea comes through the legal jargon.

BILL OF SALE OF THE SHIP OR VESSEL THE HARRIETT

APRIL 23rd 1816

Mr Thomas Mills to Mr William Phipps

Know all men in these Presents that I Thomas Mills of Savage Garden in the City of London Cornfactor assignee of the Estate and Effects of John Wash late of Old Hall in the Parish of Tollesbury... Shipowner a Bankrupt for and in consideration of the sum of ONE HUNDRED POUNDS of lawful money of Great Britain to me in hand at or before the ensealing and delivery of these presents by William Phipps of Thorpe Le Soken... mariner well and truly paid the Receipt whereof I do hereby acknowledge and myself to be therewith fully satisfied HAVE granted bargained sold assigned and absolutely grant bargain sell asign and set over unto the said William Phipps ALL that the good ship or vessel called THE HARRIETT of London... together will all... masts, sails, sail yards, anchors, cables, ropes, cords, guns, gunpowder, ammunition, small arms, tackle, apparel, boats, oars and appurtenances whatsoever... said ship or vessel has been duly registered... and a copy of the Certificate

23

of such registry is as follows...

No. 53 Certificate of British Registry. Admeasured Aground. In pursuance of an Act passed in the 26th year of... King George the 3rd... John Wash of Saint John Street Horsley Down Ship Owner having... subscribed the oath and... sworn... he is the Sole Owner of... Harriett of London whereof Abraham Nichols is at present Master and that the said ship... was formerly called Anna and Catharina taken by his Majesty's Ship Mercurius and condemned as good and lawful prize in the High Courts of Admiralty 6th Nov. 1810 and is the same Vessel mentioned in a Certificate under the Hand and Seal of the Judge of the said Court dated 8th Feb. 1812 and made free by Certificate of Freedom at London 15th Feb, 1812 and Isaac Lano acting Surveyor... having certified to us that the said Ship... is Foreign Built and has one deck and one mast... length 50 feet 6 inches... Breadth... 16 feet 2 inches... Cabin 5 feet 7 inches and admeasured 51 tons-58/94... Square Stern'd Sloop... has been duly registered at the Port of London... signed and sealed... C Welstead, J Boyce.

TO HAVE AND TO HOLD the said SHIP... unto Wm Phipps... to his... own use... for ever... IN WITNESS thereof... I... set my hand and seal the 23rd day of April... One thousand eight hundred and sixteen... Signed and sealed... in presence of Chas Druce, H Marrand. Received the day and year above written... of... Wm Phipps.

£100... received the same by me Thos Mills.

It seems therefore that the bankrupt John Wash only used the *Harriett* from February 1812, to April, 1816, and then met with financial problems. The assignee of his estate, Thomas Mills, was a corn factor and it seems likely that the ship was used in the corn trade. Life in the corn growing Sokens was frequently hard. Perhaps that is why John Wash, shipowner, went bankrupt and why Thomas Mills, cornfactor, sold a 50 ton sloop for £100. Money was safer than corn!

'Admeasured ground' simply means that the *Harriett* was laid ashore for proper examination by the Customs Surveyor. The Certificate of Freedom two years after being condemned as a lawful prize seems unusual and it is odd that she was sold in 1816 complete with armoury. It remains a mystery. Unfortunately there is no complete record of the issue of Letters of Marque (licence to act as a privateer), but one would expect her to have been registered for peaceful trading. However, she could have been smuggling, privateering or simply armed for self defence. It seems unlikely that HMS *Mercurius* would have allowed the arms to remain with the vessel after taking her as a prize. If presence of arms meant that she had, in fact, been granted Letters of Marque under John Wash's ownership, then we can assume privateering was as unsuccessful as corn trading in view of his bankruptcy.

The Captain and crew of *Mercurius* will have received a respectable reward after the sale and one wonders whether Thos Mills recouped his debts with what was left of the £100. As a rough estimate £100 in 1816 would be well over £10,000 today.

Harriett was certified as foreign built by the acting Surveyor at the Port of London Customs House. The country of origin is not mentioned, but *Anna and Catharina* would suggest a Dutch or Danish vessel.

The North Sea and East Coast swarmed with small craft privateering and the most likely explanation of the *Harriett* would seem to be that under a foreign flag as the *Anna and Catharina* she was privateering when taken as a lawful prize by HMS *Mercurius* and that John Wash, the subsequent buyer, may well have received Letters of Marque, then combining corn shipping with privateering until his bankruptcy. It is not known how the new owner, Wm Phipps, Mariner, fared with his £100 acquisition after April, 1816, nor whether the Wm Phipps, shoemaker of Kirby-le-Soken, listed in an 1848 Directory, was of the same family. His relative, John Phipps, was a shoemaker and Parish Clerk at that time. Further research might produce enlightening documents.

Many foreign prizes were bought and registered by Essex shipowners, often to replace vessels lost to the enemy. Wm Phipps may have been in this category. H A Felgate of Dovercourt, who compiled an analysis of shipowners from the registers, does not mention the *Harriett,* John Wash, Thos Mills or Wm Phipps. What befell her or them remains unknown.

By 1800 sailing barges were in their hey-day and heavier materials, such as chalk and coal, were available to bordering farms from barges via the creeks. Many Hamford quays were rebuilt in stone (Beaumont in 1830 with stone from London Bridge) to accommodate this traffic, which continued in volume until about 1920, when barges gradually declined, until virtually disappearing after the 1939/45 war.

Good roads, railways and speed were powerful competitors.

In the 1851 Census for Kirby-le-Soken 1 sailor, 6 mariners, 1 customs coast officer and 1 captain (army or marine) were listed. In the 1848 Directory Geo Lee of the Red Lion was mentioned as being master mariner and victualler. In Thorpe-le-Soken in 1851 2 fishermen and 3 mariners were noted, but

Causeway to Horsey Island at low tide

by the 1861 Census there were 5 mariners, 1 sailor, 1 seaman, 1 waterman and 1 captain, RN, on half pay: it is reasonable to suppose that most of these men would be looking to Landermere Wharf, Kirby Quay and Beaumont Quay for their occupations, with the exception of the halfpay Captain.

Farmers with land adjoining the creeks and backwaters have always had their own small boats and private jetties for local needs and for ferrying fodder to Horsey and Skippers Islands when grazing was sparse in winter. The causeway from Island Lane to Horsey needed constant attention (and still does) to keep it firm enough for carts and wagons. The ancient maps all shew a causeway from Island Lane, Kirby, to Horsey Island across the Wade. It is strange that the 1881 Ordnance Survey map shews stepping stones, as these would have been impossible for horse-drawn traffic: both earlier and later maps shew a causeway. Perhaps this was a mental aberation of the surveyor or he surveyed the area when the tide was nearly out and the uneven surface of the causeway gave the illusion of stepping stones.

The name Horsey or Horseheye is ancient, meaning horse enclosure, but in the 18th and 19th centuries the island was mainly used for sheep grazing, as was Skippers Island: it is said locally that sheep were occasionally swum across.

A fascinating and unexplained name change can be noted. Skippers Island was originally Holmes Island in the maps of John Oliver (1696), Chapman & André (1777) and Greenwood (1824), but when the area was surveyed by the Army preparing for an anticipated Napoleonic invasion and the area mobilised for civil defence, the 1805 map marked the island as Skippers or Holmes. By the 1875 Ordnance Survey it is solely Skippers and so it has remained.

A local story explains the name transition with

the romantic legend that sailing barges approaching Landermere Wharf would pause to allow the master to 'skip off' with his contraband and wait out of sight on the island, allowing the mate to berth without the skipper and clear customs before he rejoined later. A lovely tale, but surely a fictional accretion to the very real fact of smuggling in the creeks.

It seems more likely that the island was called Skippers because of the extensive and wealthy Skipper family in Kirby and district in the mid to late 18th century. From the Rent Roll of Quit Rents in 1758 John Skipper took over Holmes Island from John Hibbs at a rent of £22 per annum.

Some impression of the family can be gained from extracts of three wills deposited in the Records Office –

> John Skipper the Elder of Kirby to my eldest son John Skipper one shilling only having given him already a full share of my property... to my daughter Mary £50 of lawful money also my clock in the parlour... all the rest household goods furniture cattle corn farming stock implements in Husbandry to my youngest son Benjamin to provide for and maintain my loving wife Mary Skipper. Signed sealed 15th day of March 1789.

'One shilling' was a normal insurance in law against the will being contested.

It can be surmised that the Elder John was by this time ill, as he adds a codicil on the same day

> John Skipper the Elder of Kirby 15th March 1789. CODICIL... to his wife Mary the bed bedstead and chest of drawers and all other furniture in the parlour of room where I lay. Benjamin my son to provide for my wife during her natural life. Benjamin to pay an Annuity of £12 per year for her life.

What a significant phrase is 'where I lay'.

Another will exists of Thomas Skipper of Kirby, farmer, 1st January, 1801 –

To Sarah my dear wife all that my copyhold messuage tenement farm lands and Estate wherein I now reside and which I purchased of Mr John Cooke and also all my Freehold Barn Lands and Estate at Frinton to my wife for 14 years from the Michaelmas Day preceeding my decease. If she should so long live and continue my widow and should keep the premises in good tenantable repair and keep the buildings insured against loss or damage by fire... I do hereby charge all and every the said Estate... with the payment of the yearly sum of £30 to Ann my honoured mother in satisfaction of the yearly interest on £500... And from and after my said wife's decease or her marrying again... I give all... to my nephew John Barnard chargeable with the payment of the said annuity to my mother... if dead when nephew comes into possession then an annuity of £20 per annum to be paid to my sister Ann Barnard during her natural life.

In view of Thomas' careful reference concerning his wife Sarah keeping the estate insured and in good repair he may have had reservations about her business efficiency.

The two above wills are businesslike and without pious sentiment, however, Benjamin Skipper's will includes the traditional religious phrases, as the following extract shews

Will of Benjamin Skipper 26th January 1833. I Benjamin Skipper of Kirby... being through the blessing of God in a sound state of mind and memory but calling to mind the frail tenure of this life and that it is appointed to all men once to die, do make and ordain this

30

my last Will and Testament that is to say principally and first of all I recommend my soul into the hands of Almighty God who gave it me, and the disposal of my body I leave to the entire direction of my Friends... My worldly estate, lands, effects and all my property I give and bequeath to Mary Skipper my beloved wife. At her decease I give and bequeath to my son John Skipper 17 acres of land in the Parish of Thorpe, my property lying opposite Hog Lane... to my son Thomas Skipper £100... to my son Peter Skipper 10 acres and dwelling houses thereon in Kirby... to Benjamin my son £10.

His will is in the conventional form of an earlier age and was probably drawn up by the parish priest.

The Skipper family was reputed to have been respected by the people and were certainly well known in the area from the mid 18th century. It is a plausible suggestion that the name change about 1800 from Holmes to Skippers Island was partly a sign of this respect, as well as an indication of a well established and descriptive local designation - John Skipper's Island soon becoming Skippers Island.

So, although barge skippers may well have enjoyed 'skipping off' ship into shelter of the island with ankers of smuggled brandy, they cannot be credited with the change of name, much as the story appeals!

We can, however, compliment the Army map makers of 1805 for their astute detection of the emerging change of name. Placing Skippers first implied the common name of the time; adding Holmes acknowledged the earlier map designation. A good way of shewing their thoroughness to locals and to their superior officers.

John Skipper the Elder carefully listed his

parlour clock in his will, as clocks were valuable possessions of wealthier families and were invariably handed down from generation to generation. In his day a popular model was the one handed bracket clock illustrated, this being more suitable than the two handed long case (grandfather) clock for low ceilinged houses. A single weight sufficed for both time keeping and striking the hours and, if raised by the rope night and morning, would go for twelve hours at least. Many still survive in good working order and, although the gear wheels were filed by hand and precision engineering was by 'feel', they keep exceptionally good time. That pictured is still working in the Tendring Hundred, having been made by Richard Rayment of Bury St Edmunds in 1690.

Chapter Three

The sailing barges' function was taken over gradually by motorised vessels, many owned by small shipping companies such as the London & Rochester Sg. Co. Ltd., Metcalf Motor Coasters and F T Everard & Sons, Ltd. A few diesel engined coastal craft were indeed owned by their skippers under the Red Ensign, but many Dutch and German schoots of 230 gross and approximately 130 feet long were owned by the master buying on mortgage, with his wife as a member of the crew. Craft such as these supplanted the sailing barge of the 19th and early 20th centuries, carrying the same type of cargo. However, there is no record of any such craft ever using Kirby Quay, although they do still manage to reach The Hythe at Colchester, Mistley, Wivenhoe and Brightlingsea.

It might well be asked whether many masters in the days of sail also owned their barges. The answer is - rarely, but sometimes there was joint ownership involving perhaps two or three parties. For example, Peter Clark, who owned Kirby Quay last century, entered into a tripartite arrangement whereby Charles Appleby (born in Thorpe, but a resident of Kirby for 13 years) owned half of one vessel, Peter Clark owned half of two vessels and Captain Ford half of one: all used in the corn trade.

Charles Appleby was master of one of these in 1814 and in 1820 applied for ownership of part of that vessel, but being unable to raise the money, his associate Peter Clark, who probably needed financial assistance, not only sold the vessel, but also the wharf. It seems strange today that Appleby, a master mariner in work, could not raise the £50/75 needed to buy a share in the ship he commanded, but this was before the days of the Big Five Banks full of helpful, caring managers! Banking, as we know it, was only just emerging in the early 19th century. Many banks, rapidly to fade, were started by small tradesmen in market towns and a large number failed in the commercial crises of the times. The French Wars imposed a great strain on the English monetary system and the Government's Order in Council of 1797 forbidding the Bank of England to pay its notes in gold was confirmed by Parliament, continuing in force until 1821. Reserves were allowed to fall to dangerous levels by 1825 before any protective action was taken.

The unfortunate Charles Appleby probably found local banks jittery and unco-operative in 1820. He might well have wished he lived in Tudor times when London scriveners (lawyers specialising in drawing up contracts and lending money) were still operating. We shall never know how he fared when bereft of the north easterly winds in his face and without the heavy lurch of a laden vessel at his feet.

Kirby Quay was, until early this century, an important asset to the community. For instance, William George Clark Warner, tenant of Devereux Farm, Kirby, from 1823 to 1862 would be glad of the unloading facilities, as he is described as farmer and coal merchant. A steady flow of sailing colliers from the north east plied the East Coast routes,

3 4

penetrating as far inland as possible to avoid the expense of wagon transport. Some even reached Sudbury via the River Stour.

A Bill of Sale of 1824 described the Kirby Quay district as 'an area abounding with hares and partridge. The Quay or Wharfe connecting Mercantile business with a farming concern... capable of containing two vessels... on the Wharfe is a Corn Granary, Dwelling House, Counting House, Lime Kiln and Lime House, Store House, Stable and enclosed Coal Yard'. William White in 1848 describing Kirby-le-Soken mentions 'Kirby Quay where corn, etc., is shipped'. So the Wharf was important to the parish.

A brickworks was built in 1899 to the west of Quay Lane and offered for sale 5 August, 1903, together with cottages and building plots in the undeveloped Quay Lane. One sales' point was that the site was near Kirby Quay 'where building materials etc., can be loaded and unloaded'. Other particulars indicate the anticipated prospects of the times. The Island View Estate, as it was called, was described as –

adjoining the popular and rising seaside and health resorts of Walton-on-Naze and Frinton-on-Sea... pleasantly situated in one of the prettiest districts on the East Coast, with charming views of the Handford Waters and Islands, where splendid yachting, boating, fishing and wildfowl shooting is obtainable. The Estate is within easy walking distance of Walton and Frinton, approached by a capital service of trains; and steamers run daily during the season between Walton, London, Ipswich, Harwich, Clacton and Yarmouth... an exceptional opportunity is afforded Brick Merchants, Speculators and others, of acquiring a thoroughly sound business, as the trade of the Yard has steadily increased every year since its opening four years ago, whilst there is every reason to believe the property will rapidly increase in value in the near future. The Yard turns out a high quality brick, which, as it becomes known in the district, is becoming increasingly popular, and with the growing districts of Walton and Frinton a steady and convenient market is assured: 132,000 bricks have already been burnt this season, and 115,000 facing bricks sold at varying prices from 31 shillings to 33 shillings per thousand at the Yard. Cottages are in great demand in the district. The building sites are the remaining portion of the Island View Estate and afford the last opportunity of acquiring land on the Estate.

Incidentally, another brickworks existed at this time to the west of Witton Wood Road, Frinton, the owner and workers living in Upper Fourth Avenue. The houses are still there today.

Bricks, being heavy, would be a regular export from Kirby Quay.

Before the rents available from the existing cottages in Quay Lane at the turn of the century are noted, it is interesting to compare them with those for the Soken Manors in the 16th century. Rent for the Manors was £29.12.6¾d. Rectories and other premises in Thorpe, Kirby and Walton were £11.16.0d per annum. Wage rates were about eight old pence a day for carpenters, 4d for labourers and 6½ pence for masons (in 1957 average wages were £12.10.0d. and in 1988 £190 a week).

In 1903 the 12 cottages in Quay Lane, Kirby, produced a total of £110.10.0d in rents. At the turn of the century £1 a week was considered a respectable wage, many familes having to make do on substantially less. Producing about £9 a cottage

Watercolour of 1900. Kirby Quay with hay barge

Victorian photograph shewing Kirby Quay Corn Granary

in a year's rent would require careful planning by the tenant.

When Captain Jim Uglow, MBE, Barge Master for Everards of Greenhithe, ran away to sea at the age of 14 in 1920 and was taken on as cook on the sailing barge *Glenmore* (built in 1903), his wages, even as late as this, were only twelve shillings a week, plus food, but less any breakages. When barges were prolific in all small ports and quays last century the wages were even less.

Basically, there were two types of barge, the Channel barges and the Essexmen, the latter mostly worked the East Coast and came to Hamford Water. When trade slacked off they would 'go seeking' in the English Channel. A good and experienced barge master had many contacts and could generally smell out prospective business. He also made sure the owners knew where to find him, so that fresh instructions could be speedily followed up. Thames barge skippers would refer to the Essexmen contemptuously as 'Reed sparrows' or 'Butterflies'.

Few skippers of either type used charts: maps were printed in their memories. Compasses were installed, but generally shoals, eddies, tides, winds, beacons and landmarks were preferred and, probably in view of vast practical experience, safer. We speak today of air pilots flying by the seat of their pants; barge skippers sailed by the soles of their feet, making vital judgements intuitively and on massive experience of every type of hazard in all weathers.

Craft using Kirby Quay were mainly Essexmen and well used to hugging the coastline, often spending days or weeks at anchor or tied up, waiting for favourable conditions or cargo. A surviving Victorian watercolour shews a coastal barge loading hay at Kirby Quay and an Edwardian photograph depicts a barge waiting for cargo. An earlier Victorian photograph shews the Corn Granary on

Edwardian photograph of Granary, barge and Pilot's Cottage.
Note window and door in Granary, by now lived in

Quay being jacked up 5 feet to avoid flooding

the west of the Quay. Some idea of the change of use of the granary can be seen by examining the pictures in date order. The earliest shews the granary without windows and only a large loading door and small door; the next omits the doors, shewing a window at the west end; the photograph including barge, granary and Pilot's Cottage is interesting because by the now the window has curtains and the door includes a letter box and steps. Presumably half the granary was being used as living accommodation just prior to the 1914/18 War. Between the wars the whole building was converted to a private dwelling house: a sale advertisement in the *Evening Gazette*, 7 March, 1980, said, 'Historic Quay House for sale, plus $7\frac{1}{2}$ acres. Dates back to the 16th century. Then used as a tidal granary. Private Creek and Slipway. Quay House mentioned in Arthur Ransome's book *Secret Waters*, there referred to as 'Witches' Quay'. 4 beds. 2 Receps. Kit/Break/Rm. Bathroom and Cloakroom.'

Modern photographs shew Quay House being jacked up 5 feet to avoid the foundations flooding. A small motorised vessel can be seen moored bow first. In 1824 two commercial sailing barges could berth at the same time, moored stern first.

The transition from 19th century sail to modern engine obviously took place gradually. According to Mr R Hutchings, now of Walton but previously from Kirby, at the age of 11 or 12 he steered the very last sailing barge into Kirby Quay as late as 1922, under the direction of the pilot, Bill Scone, who lived in Pilot's Cottage. He thinks the boat was called *British Empire* and that she is now restored and preserved for posterity elsewhere. He also says that in the same year the granary at Kirby Quay was bought by Mr Pearce, a plasterer from Clacton, who converted the building into a house: the corn trade was finished, but the building was too good

40

Silhouette of a
Thames Spritsail
Barge. Normally just
over 100 tons and
crewed by 2 men and
sometimes a boy.

Those in good condition had sails removed and diesel
engines installed early in the 20th century.

Then came the gradual development of the small
motor coaster. Many were Dutch and called 'Schoot'
[pronounced Scoot].

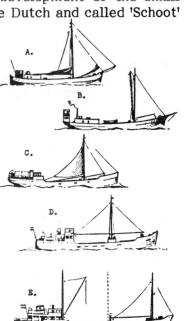

A. Early auxiliary type.
Koff rig. Built 1910. 90
feet long. 130 tons gross
B. Converted schooner.
Built 1910. Length 100
feet. 148 tons gross
C. Built 1921. Length
110 feet. 200 tons gross
D. Built 1938. Length
125 feet. 280 tons gross.
Note that by now with
a higher bridge and
cruiser stern
E. Built 1946. Length 155
feet. 450 tons gross. This
still popular type has an
increased rake of stem
and a larger mass aft.

Steel construction sailing barges were still being
built,in the 1920s, but most were soon converted to
diesel power.

Sailing barge **Pudge** off Mistley

Waterdale, registered Rju

to ignore. He has no knowledge of any motorised barges ever using Kirby Quay subsequently and asserts the late 20s marked the end of the quay as a small local wharf, private yachts being the only visitors from then until now.

The most active and still prosperous shipping company still engaged in coastal and continental shipping is F T Everard of Greenhithe. Most East Coast ports and small quays have been familiar to them for many years. They, more than any, have assisted the change-over from sail to engine this century and have been most helpful in providing details of surviving records: three in particular are worth quoting in illustration of this evolution.

As their office record sheet states, a 3 masted schooner the *Grana*, built in 1918 and purchased by them in 1920 was motorised during the next two years and, after trading under their house flag, was sold to John D Sullivan of Southend in 1935: before then the name had been changed to *Capable*.

The sailing barge *Alf Everard* of steel construction, built in Fellows yard, Great Yarmouth in 1925 was converted to motor ship in 1943 and sunk in the Thames Estuary (no cause given) in 1953. Another steel barge, the *Fred Everard*, built in Great Yarmouth in 1926, was converted to a motor ship in 1938 and, still trading, she sank off Margate in 1956.

So, although commercial sailing barge traffic ceased in 1922 at Kirby Quay, the actual change from sail to engine took many years before sailing barges were used purely for nostalgic races and pleasure cruises.

The London & Rochester Trading Company Ltd. (now Crescent Shipping Ltd.) was formed by George William Gill of Chatham in 1858 and, by the end of the 19th century, a fleet of trading barges had been acquired, trading round the coast with miscellaneous

43

cargoes, especially cement and bricks. Mr Hutchings remembers bricks arriving at Kirby Quay for the sea walls when he was a boy in the 1920s. Their shallow draft made it possible to navigate small little depth creeks and thus discharge cargo at conveniently placed quays such as Landermere, Beaumont and Kirby.

Crescent now have only one sailing barge, the *Cabby,* built in 1928. Fully refurbished, but with the addition of an engine, she is still alive and well for charter as a conference centre, school trips or business and club pleasure cruises.

Apart from *Cabby,* a few sailing barges are also maintained by Everards for Thames Sailing Barge Races, but the extensive commercial fleets of both Crescent and Everards are now all motor vessels and too large for Hamford Water and the creeks.

Thus ended an era.

Sailing Barge Cabby

Coastal mariners' clothing was varied and often
comprised 'Sunday best' being used up. Many a
double breasted all wool indigo serge suit finished
its days on the barges, changing colour from navy
blue to shiny greenish grey in the process. But there
was an accepted style of working clothes for every
occupation and those in funds would buy purpose
built garments specifically for work.

Before the days of welded seam PVC waterproof
clothing, oilskin trousers, jackets and sou'westers
were essential: cotton based, black or yellow, they
were impregnated with boiled linseed oil, making
them both stiff and strong smelling, but remaining
as waterproof as modern PVC unless folded and
stored for any length of time, when they tended to
crack, leak or remain stuck together.

The vital and universal garments directly underneath were either the well-worn and therefore
relegated to second-best melton or serge reefer
jackets or, failing that, seamen's jerseys. The latter
were all wool (oiled) navy or navy and white
speckled, long sleeved and with various traditional
designs. Styles, handed down for centuries, were
carefully preserved by hand-knitters to such effect

that invariably a man's origins and occupation could be deduced from his jersey. Guernsey or Franklin varieties were virtually double fronted in view of the heavy wind cheating patterns on the chest.

The chest patterns were originally incorporated to give extra protection from the elements, but because of the extra wool they were more expensive. Other popular jerseys were of 2 ply wool in plain stitch navy blue wool with either square, rolled, crew or stand collars. These, essential for warmth, were always heavily oiled. Retailers' stocks, wrapped in brown paper parcels, needed no labels as the oil shewed through in dark patches and the smell was unmistakable. Many seasoned mariners avoided washing jerseys so as to retain the warmth-giving oil as long as practical.

Under the jersey shirts would either be navy blue cotton drill or double fronted collarless Oxford shirts, white with black stripes. Beneath were long-sleeved button fronted woollen or fleecy cotton (cheaper) vests with matching long pants; not with elastic waists, but button fronted with tape loops to hook over trouser braces. For the cutting north-east winds all wool flannel square necked vests were popular, the best being made by Johnson & Sons of Great Yarmouth, who continued in business until the middle years of this century. As all housewives know, untreated wool shrinks in washing, so flannel vests were cut generously to allow for shrinkage. For instance, a size 42" chest vest, when new, would measure no less than 65": even then a seaman would come into the shop complaining that his flannel vests no longer covered his navel.

Many items of mercantile clothing were made in large quantities in Great Yarmouth, Grimsby, Lowestoft, Plymouth and Liverpool, but many smaller ports also supported manufacturers, some of whom used local housewives as outworkers.

Trousers were often worn out Sunday best, but might have been bought specially, particularly by deep sea men. In warm weather navy blue cotton drill (dungarees) at 2/-[10p] were worn: in colder weather woollen serge or melton trousers for under £1 were normal. A thick cotton trouser for all seasons was gambroon, popularly called 'pepper & salt', because of its speckled grey and white: these were frequently lined with unbleached cotton for extra warmth.

If going ashore, navy blue melton trousers (32 ozs per square yard) with matching reefer jacket or, for well established barge skippers, the same but in all wool indigo serge, which, with care, would last almost a lifetime, maybe looking rather green and shiny towards the end.

By 1900 younger crew members were attracted by American denim, a desirable hard wearing cloth, easy to wash and dry. Jackets were available for well under £1. Originally made from 15 ounces to the square yard cloth and very tough, they were the subject of exploitation by unscrupulous manufacturers, who found that, by adding glue, they could make a 10 ounce cloth feel like 15 ounce at the same price. Washing soon disclosed the subterfuge, but by then the wearer was well out in the North Sea. Had the heavy glue smell been detected this could be explained as part of the American method of manufacture.

At sea nightwear was whatever was left dry underneath outer garments or, if calm or at anchor, at home or on the spree, nightshirts, knee length in Oxford shirt striped material or even in woollen flannel. Pyjamas had not yet arrived from the Mohammedans and glamour was unimportant at sea or on short visits home with candle lit bedrooms.

Several times a year (sometimes prompted by foreign infestations of bugs and fleas) the seamen would buy a new 'Donkey's breakfast' from the nearest shop. This was a striped cotton twill mattress cover filled with hay or straw to make bunks more comfortable at sea. Often these hung outside the shop as enticements or reminders.

Socks were thick wool in light grey (called army grey for some unknown reason) or navy blue for boots, and long white oiled wool for sea boots. Oiled wool socks are still available today, but mainly used by fell walkers or climbers. At sea they were infrequently washed as generally freshened by sea water and hung from strings to dry from bulkheads there was no time for finesse. There is a record of one seaman, in warm calm weather placing his dirty socks in a bucket of water under his bunk preparatory to proper washing and finding after a few days that fermentation had begun.

Normally, any working man's occupation was recognisable from his clothing. Nobody on the quayside could confuse a man from the barges with one from the land. Labourers unloading barges invariably would be wearing corduroy trousers in fawn, dark brown or Norfolk drab (grey/green): all colours lightened after repeated washing, the fawn becoming almost white. The strong glue smell of new cloth disappeared after one wash and the trousers hung better without the stiffening. The trousers were always tied under the knee with string to avoid muddying from boots.

Another popular cloth was moleskin (nothing to do with the animal) in fawn or dark brown. Both corduroy and moleskin were tightly woven heavy cotton cloth and just about windproof. A material much used for both trousers and jackets was grey or, occasionally, fawn, Derby tweed in thick wool and cotton mixtures, the best cloth coming from Hebden Bridge, Yorkshire.

Whatever cloth was used for working suits,

5 High Street, Gravesend, 1914. Hilda Collins in doorway.
Dungarees at 3/3d; tailor made suits at 45/-

designs were similar. Moleskin trousers, because of the thick intractable nature of the cloth, tended to be simpler in design and specification, but Derby tweed suits, for instance, could be ordered with one, two or three rows of stitching around lapels, jacket edges, sleeves and even trouser bottoms. These were not fads, but to improve wearing capacity. Often trouser bottoms, always plain and never with turn-ups, would have as many as five rows of obvious heavy stitching. For extra protection Derby tweed jackets were frequently ordered with shoulder yokes of double material with two or three points at the back, sometimes double stitched.

Trousers in all three cloths had two inch belt loops to take hide belts with heavy brass buckles, plus braces' buttons. The higher waist line at the back was for extra warmth when bending. No buttoned flies were fitted, but ingenious flaps at the front sufficed, opening from both sides to crutch level, aptly called 'whole falls'. The heavy belts had little connection with keeping the trousers up, often they served purely as supports for overhanging stomachs: when men's outfitters were measuring up customers they said, "Do you want the belt above or below the corporation?".

Mostly, working trousers were lined with unbleached cotton with extra strong pockets of the same material under the drop front and frequently with one smaller pocket, inset, for the silver 'turnip' watch and key. Creases were not ironed into trousers, the material and the lining being too thick: they really did look like stovepipes.

All men's outfitters carried stocks of ready-made working suits in chest sizes 38 to 46 inches, other sizes to special order. Cuffs were specified for extra wear and firmly stitched to the sleeves. Being of good quality cloth such suits would last for years. Never being subjected to modern dry-cleaning they 'stiffened' with the years and lasted a long time, aided by the shine of grease.

Matching waistcoats had long backs for protection in heavy cotton drill and sleeve lining were also in this material.

Seamen in serge or melton reefer jackets and labourers in Derby tweed three piece suits would both wear a knotted red kerchief in place of a tie when going out. Patterns of white dots were traditional and many buyers were fussy as to the exact pattern on their red 'neckerchiefs'.

Considering the low wages, clothing was not cheap for labourers or bargemen; it was, however, by today's standards, excellent quality. Indigo serge suits in heavy cloth were tailor made for two guineas and guaranteed to stand all weathers. Readymade heavy melton double-fronted overcoats were £2. A quart of gin or whisky to fit capacious inner pockets could be bought for 13p, brandy (for toothache) 25p a quart for old French or just under 40p for Rouyer Guillet – unless, of course, one had special access to a smuggling pub.

Even though tooth extractions by a dentist were only 5p a tooth or 10p with anaesthetic, when related to wages of less than £1 a week and bearing in mind the cruder methods of dentistry practiced last century, it can be appreciated why brandy was often preferred. Bargemen and labourers alike undoubtedly suffered more than we do with our teeth, but with feet it was different. Fashionable, uncomfortable styles in footwear had not yet arrived; durability and practical comfort were all important. Sea boots were stout and in leather, needing only regular greasing for waterproofing. Comfort was assured as most boots were handmade and to measure: factory made boots and shoes were beginning to emerge by mid-century, but were considered inferior, as indeed they were.

In the Kirby Census of 1851 there were three shoemakers listed, but in the 1848 *Directory* there had been six. In Thorpe-le-Soken there was one bootmaker and one shoemaker in 1851 and in 1861 four bootmakers and eight shoemakers (one being deaf and dumb).

One cannot help wondering whether the Census taker in Kirby was as thorough as he might have been in 1851 as no tailor is listed, but Thomas Theobald, tailor, is shewn in the *Directory*. It is unlikely that Kirby bargemen would have to go as far as Thorpe for clothing on a regular basis, as Kirby shopkeepers, like all small traders, knew local requirements intimately and were most happy to stock a large and varied range of goods, even if they could only afford to stock a few garments in each range. Small establishments were well served by wholesalers and the smallest would still be welcome at any Colchester warehouse even though he never made bulk purchases. It was possible for him to buy two shirts, four pairs of socks and two pairs of braces. Prices were always per dozen and it was the convention to order the above as two twelfth shirts, four twelfth socks and two twelfth braces: even a single garment was one twelfth.

Profits were small and turnover of stock on some items might be only once a year. An article bought at ten shillings [50p] would be sold for 14/11d. In drapery the fifteen shillings article would be sold for fourteen shillings and elevenpence three farthings: the farthing off was supposed – and presumably did – tempt the housewife. If the draper was faced with giving a farthing in change, a packet of pins was offered instead. A dozen such transactions would produce an extra profit of one penny (or less). No shopkeeper would ever say the price was fourteen shillings and eleven pence three farthings, it was always fourteen eleven three.

Needless to say, unless the purchase was as important as ordering a suit, boots or oilskins, the seaman would entrust buying to his wife; she was more impressed with pins and farthings, in any case!

In larger ports, had a visiting seaman been spending hard earned money on wine and women, it was not unusual for the woman of the moment to steer him to a seaman's outfitter for essential mercantile clothing before the money ran out, in which case the shopkeeper kept a stock of women's cheap headscarves or handkerchiefs to give her to reward such public spirited and profitable behaviour.

Although by the early 19th century Telford and Macadam had revolutionised the surface of main roads and, therefore, road transport, Quay Lane was only of gravel even in Edwardian days. Wagons holding 30 to 40 cwt would trundle and crunch their way to the Street, Kirby-le-Soken, and thence to farms and industrial concerns nearby. Every pound weight of barge cargo had to be hand winched from the hold and manhandled to the wagons. Very often crews found they simply exchanged sea water soaked clothing for sweat soaked when they berthed.

By present day standards, food to fuel this expenditure of energy was plentiful; lacking in finesse, but gaining in bulk and calories. A typical example on a three handed sailing barge in harbour, after having stocked up, would be a large piece of rib of beef or leg of mutton with two vegetables one day and remains fried the next. In addition, a huge boiled currant or similar pudding, also sliced and fried or eaten cold the next day. Invariably a fore-end of bacon cut in $\frac{1}{4}$ inch slices when at anchor or at sea, weather permitting. Most barges had a salt crock with anything up to 20 pounds of beef flank preserved.

If calm enough at sea it was cook one day, fry up or eat cold the next. Sometimes a meat pudding

Quay Lane. The old granary, now Quay House, just visible

would be boiled for four hours in a two gallon cast iron pot. When the bread was used up, ship's biscuits tapped free of weevils sufficed, but even prolonged dunking in tea failed to make them attractive. Should a few vegetables remain after a few days at sea, these were boiled in the same pot at the same time as the pudding. Only tea was drunk at sea: beer, of course, in quantities in port. Barge owners' fresh instructions for cargo contracts would be delivered to crews waiting in the nearest public houses. North Sea breezes soon cured hangovers.

Whilst sailing, all on board were on duty, more often than not soaked through and only sleeping in calm weather or when waiting at anchor for a berth or cargo. Large helpings of solid protein were essential and expected.

Barge skippers themselves always organised buying of food before sailing and the Red Lion inn-keeper in 1848, George Lee, being a retired master mariner, would be an obvious choice when stocking a vessel.

Access to shops and inns was convenient from Kirby Creek as for centuries there had been three land routes to Lower Kirby; Maltings Lane passing Marsh House overlooking the sea wall, Quay Lane, and Island Lane from the low tide Horsey Island crossing. Smugglers favoured the less populated footpaths.

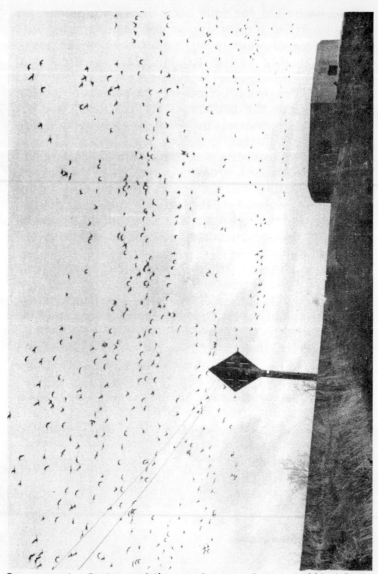

One seventh of the world's population of dark bellied Brent
geese winter in the area.

Chapter Five

Wildfowl - Wildfowlers - Taxidermists - Gamekeepers

Apart from local and commercial traffic there was much activity by wildfowlers, trappers of birds and egg collectors. By far the most significant development for Hamford Water bird life was the invention in France of the flintlock in the early 17th century, which by mid century had been vastly improved to replace all others. Cartridges were in standard use by the 18th century and were deadly to birds. The percussion lock replaced the flintlock by 1825, being more reliable in wet or windy weather. Cartridges with their own ignition systems were introduced and continual improvements took place until Mr Boxer, late in the century, introduced a central section to the cartridge which crushed easily against the firing compound: so the modern cartridge was perfected to complete the menace to wildfowl.

Between 1860 and 1900 the muzzle-loading gun was replaced by breech-loading, self-ejecting, hammerless guns - the modern shotgun had arrived.

Some species of bird disappeared altogether: many were shot only to be stuffed and cased in domed glass on the mantlepiece or in the china cabinet, especially if very rare and therefore prestigious. So popular was the sport that many landowners employed gamekeepers to encourage and husband breeding game birds and to decimate the birds of prey. The increase in the numbers of gamekeepers in the first half of the last century was phenomenal, as was the use of spring traps, pole traps, nets and poisoned baits for 'vermin', such as stoat, weasel, fox, red squirrel, crow, jay and magpie. Some gamekeepers were required to swear an oath, "I shall use my best endeavours to destroy all birds of prey with their nests wherever they can be found. So help me God.".

Collectors also preyed on bird life, reaching a peak of activity in late Victorian times. Ideally, they got a male and female bird, young and eggs, plus nest: taxidermy flourished. Some birds were trapped and sold in osier cages in the nearest town to remind townees of their recently lost rural past.

The arable fields in Kirby teemed with partridges before modern methods of cultivation destroyed habitats. Last century red legged French partridges, introduced in 1763 by the Earl of Rochford and released in Essex, could be seen in Kirby, but not in company with the common partridge, as they do not mix. Pesticides, plus shooting, have reduced the latter more than the introduced birds: the common partridge chicks are more dependent on insects.

Pheasants were brought to England by the Romans and were largely ignored for centuries, but were vastly increased in numbers by estate owners breeding for sport as shotguns were perfected. The so-called 'Pheasant Era' was 1880/1914. The Victorian local name for this decorative bird was 'ole long tail'. A record bag of the times was 3,945 shot in Scotland in one day: the estate record book for the following year bemoans that numbers of birds 'seem to be decreasing'.

A wet spring reducing hatching could mean a poor shooting season and gamekeepers having less game to preserve for slaughter were anxious to appear to 19th century landlords/sportsmen to be working hard and would therefore maintain gruesomely bedecked gibbets to prove it. Hanging corpses of kestrels, buzzards, marsh harriers, peregrines, sparrow hawks and owls were displayed as evidence of hard work, despite their predations on game being relatively negligible.

No wonder that, by 1914, the bird population was at an all time low, especially around Hamford Water. Any bird with a hooked beak became rare, as did wild game birds. The 1914/18 War gave respite and after the war collecting eggs and the stuffing of birds slowly went out of fashion.

Until 1760 hunting in and around the Sokens consisted in the main of one man, one dog, one gun and a few snares: comparatively harmless in view of the teeming wildlife existing in each parish. Then came the Enclosure Acts, with the resulting hedge-rows: common land became private and birds, rabbits and hares with them. The villager previously relying on snaring, trapping and shooting for his modest pot was transformed into a poacher. He was harassed by the iniquitous Game Laws, man-traps for the unwary and colonial penal settlements in Australia for the unlucky.

A further hazard was that Victorian and Edwardian ladies favoured brightly coloured plumes of feathers for hats and fans. Many a kingfisher met an end in Hamford Water for its brilliant blue plumage, as did great crested grebes, which were drastically culled. Many a packet of colourful feathers found its way to London via Colchester and the creeks were more drab as a result.

So fashion, sportsmen, collectors, ðologists, gamekeepers, feather merchants, all had an effect on birds in the 19th century, but there were other factors also at work - manmade, of course. The corncrake bred naturally in Tendring until it began to decline rapidly from 1860: this contraction has been attributed to the mechanisation of farming and the earlier cutting of hay. The harsh 'grated comb' song, although far from beautiful except to a lonely female corncrake, would nevertheless remind locals of wildlife sharing Kirby meadows and its passing by the turn of the century would help to mark a traumatic change in a way of life caused by emerging farm machinery and methods.

In this present age of conservation it is hard to imagine the wholesale slaughter of waterfowl in Hamford Water in the past. Anything that moved was shot, the rarer the better. If the flesh was unpalatable, the skin could always be stuffed - and was. So, birds prized today and rejoiced over through binoculars were shot on sight in the backwaters; for example, bean and pink footed geese, white-tailed geese (especially on Horsey Island), Brent geese in their thousands (in 1860 32 punt gunners, firing simultaneously, shot 704 on Dengie Flats), shelduck, widgeon, teal, mallard, pintail, eider, long-tailed duck, goldeneye, smew, red-breasted merganser, goosander, quail, golden and grey plover, purple sandpiper, dunlin, godwit, curlew and redshank. Undoubtedly many other species were destroyed, including occasional migrants blown off-course by adverse winds.

Identification of rare birds was carried out with great enthusiasm, but always over a carcase. Victorian ornithologists were keen and informed, but before the advent of high speed film, telescopic lenses and colour prints, a glass case full of stuffed birds became a visual reference source.

The salty air of Hamford Water no longer continually resounds to sounds of shot guns, as it did a hundred years ago, and several wildfowlers' punts rot away quietly in the backwaters. Wildlife is reviving and, in many cases, flourishing as, fortunately for them, man does not grow crops or use machines and lethal chemicals on beaches or salt flats. Apart from the menace of invading oil pollution and occasional sewage from Harwich and Dovercourt creeping into the sheltered waters of Hamford, mudflat creatures are undisturbed.

Gamekeepers are now a rare breed in the large open fields of Tendring Hundred and the Sokens, many farmers having to keep their own eyes open for the occasional poacher of pheasant, partridge, rabbit or hare. In the acute rural poverty of the early 19th century, however, and with the 1831 Game Laws provoking violence on a scale rivalling the unrest of the years after Waterloo, numerous gamekeepers lived dangerous lives. Between 1833 and 1844 no less than 42 gamekeepers were reported killed by poachers at a time when a labourer's family lived on one shilling a day and a pheasant would sell in the open market for five shillings. Despair and poverty are overwhelming driving forces on normally law abiding folk.

Previous 'live and let live' policies of farmers towards the occasional local transgressor who kept within reasonable bounds inevitably fostered the belief that ancient customs were also ancient rights and desperate assertion of these resulted in bloodshed. A resurgence of this, plus naked financial motives, can be seen today in the growing poaching of deer and salmon in other parts of the country, attended by physical violence towards hapless gamekeepers or water bailiffs. Sadly, it appears that the motive is money rather than hardship. Some would say a reflection of our times.

The Victorian sportsman may have assisted the
decline of wildlife, but he did not damage the plants
of the Sokens. Today the waterfowl are increasing
in Hamford Water, but indigenous flora is rapidly
dying out. Progress in mechanization, drainage,
chemical fertilizers and pesticides have turned
arable fields and borders into a scene a Kirby
inhabitant from last century would not recognise
as the environment he knew intimately.

That spectacular plant, the poppy, with its
brilliant red flowers sprinkling every corn field with
cheer, is now rare. Poppies favour newly disturbed
ground and the seeds survive in soil for generations,
but cannot cope with herbicides. Rare, too, are once
proloific corn cockle, corn marigold, heartsease,
scarlet pimpernel, red bartsia and rest harrow.
Unlike the poppy, which still appears occasionally
from ancient buried seed after soil disturbance, they
will not return unless farming methods revert.

Hedgerows and woodland borders are no longer
ablaze with violet, primrose, cowslip and town hall
clock: they have gone missing with their habitats.
Fortunately cowslips are making a come-back beside
motorways, including the A12 to the west of

Tendring Hundred. The unmolested seeds are air—borne in the draught from traffic and, with public access prohibited, they flourish.

Kirby's once rich grazing and hay meadows are now sown with fodder grass and regular ploughing and re-seeding is eliminating even the buttercup. Any hedges left are no longer layered, but hacked by mechanical flails, leaving torn and shredded twigs and gaps at the base. The superbly cut and laid hedges of old, apart from acting as wind-breaks, stock fences and habitats for flora and fauna, also harboured insect predators and birds, both keeping pests in check naturally. It is true that crop yields were two thirds lower, but so were costs and 'mountains' were only things to be climbed.

Additionally, without farm chemical run-off, the channels, fleets and borrow-dykes (channels remaining after removal of earth for sea walls) were pollution free and waving with that graceful reed, phragmites, much favoured by bearded tits, reed warblers and reed buntings. The tits still survive to the north of Dunwich, while warblers and buntings can still be seen in reed beds seaward of Frinton Golf Course.

In late summer, when Hamford mud was exposed, drying waterways were full of common, green and wood sandpipers. Now, a century later, only a few isolated sites remain and phragmites-loving birds maintain a precarious existance. At least they are spared the shooting dangers their ancestors endured.

Victorian and Edwardian courting couples, when strolling in the quiet Soken lanes, would be familiar with numerous hedgerow birds nesting, feeding and singing in the dense and varied hedges. Today it is an event to see flocks of goldfinches and linnets, although they remain in good quantity in the scrub at the Naze. Here again, they are at least free from the perils of netting and trapping by song-bird catchers, who sold caged birds to town dwellers.

Wildlife, plants, herbs, superstitions, legends and history were only of passing interest to Kirby bargemen. Such information was doubtless absorbed at mother's knee or in a Dame School held in a private house with 10 to 30 pupils with fees from 3d to 9d a week.

Last century cottagers with children at home would have vases filled with a wide variety of meadow and hedgerow flowers on the window sill, with kitchens sporting drying bunches of locally gathered herbs for 'do it yourself' doctoring. Today a herb gatherer, unless assiduous and experienced, could return home empty handed from marshes, dykes and fields around Hamford Water.

In times past the next step from herb remedies was to resort to witches. Now they are only memories or subjects for bed-time stories, many no doubt based on handed down facts about the notorious 'Witch Hunter General' Matthew Hopkins of Manningtree, who sent several supposed witches – generally innocent and lonely old women or those ill-favoured in looks or eccentric in habit – to their deaths in the Tendring area in 1645/7. Nevertheless, 'wise' women, Widow or Old Mother So-and-So, would still exercise influence where illness or romantic problems existed a century ago. Even as late as 1910 Mrs Jackson, late of Kirby, in her unpublished memoirs, states of her early childhood, "The nearest doctor lived at Thorpe-le-Soken and rode in a pony and trap to visit his patients". The implication from the context was that it was all a bit of a bother to call him out all that way because, "One old lady in the village made and sold her own ointment and always a carton of this was found in most households, what I remember of it, it looked like pure lard, but it healed any wound".

Locally, carrots were still recommended to cure

gall-stones, asthma, eye trouble and rheumatism. Freshly infused elder flowers were used for eye complaints (the essence is still used today in non-prescriptive eye lotion), but it was unlucky to have elder flowers indoors as it was firmly believed that the Holy Cross was made from elder wood, that Judas hanged from it and that witches used it: ancient folklore surviving from the Celts believed the elder to be a sacred tree. The specie was perhaps maligned because horses refused it and the smell of crushed leaves was rank.

No bright young thing wishing to cheer up an overworked mother, would dream of taking may blossom into the house from any Kirby lane before May Day. Witches brooms were said to be made of may and no knowledgeable witch would enter a house if a stranger had nailed a branch in the loft – a legend unlikely to be tested very often one would think! But if may was nailed in the cowshed the cows would give more milk than usual: they probably did in fact, because when the may is out there is more grass about as well. However, traditions were strong and the smell is so pungent it was better to leave may blossom alone.

Children and teenagers, with extensive sky-scape views, especially over Hamford Water's expanse of horizon and after experiencing dramatic thunderstorms rending the heavens over Horsey and Skippers Islands, would place acorns on the window sill to save them from thunderbolts – a relic of appeasing the Sky God. Woe betide them should an owl look through the window as a death would follow at night.

With thicker undergrowth before this century, snails were plentiful. Yearning maidens would put a snail on a slate during the night of 20th May and read the slime traced initials of a future lover when dawn broke. The really love-sick maiden with her own bedroom or sharing with sympathetic sisters would suspend her stays with a garter on the wall and, without taking eyes off the garment, walk backwards when, hopefully, the apparition of her future lover would materialise as she fell into bed. Immediate problems were avoided at the crucial moment and position of surrender, as the apparition faded in the mists of Victorian decorum.

Should this experiment prove unsuccessful, the next best was to eat a small may leaf on Midsummer's Eve in order to dream of the future spouse. When he came in the flesh, respectably clothed of course, a test of his future faithfulness was for her to tickle the inside of her nostrils by bruised yarrow (an older name was sneezewort): if blood could be induced he would be faithful, but when they became lovers, bad luck would follow any eating of yarrow.

For the better educated romantics there was a recognised language of flowers. Many an amorous message without words could be sent by carefully selected flower bouquets. Larkspur indicated the 'lightness of a lark': woe betide the enthusiast who sent them to a more than comfortably buxom wench. Cowslips signified 'winning grace'; if not misunderstood, the next floral offering could be golden rod as these 'whisper a tale of hope to fancy's child'. With such an ambiguous sentiment and if she happened to be quick in spotting a possible double meaning, a hasty bunch of daffodils would shew 'regret': following up with variegated tulips for 'beautiful eyes' might cement the liaison.

Great tact and intuitive understanding of the maiden would be required before sending mignonette which said 'your qualities surpass your charms': she might think her skill with suet puddings was more prized than sex appeal. If everything went wrong and a rebuff was delivered a bunch of hydrangeas for 'heartlessness' might stir her gentle conscience.

If this failed sweet peas for 'departure' signified dignified withdrawal. The really spiteful could always close flower and every other type of communication with a posy of ice plant flowers saying 'your looks freeze me'. The spurned, but lusty and hopeful youth could then keep his roving eye open for any girl clutching a handful of flowering grasses for 'submission'.

Life could be elegantly interesting with tantalising and genteel suggestions proferred to avoid vulgarity in any romantic intrigue.

Some wild Hamford Water plants were once of social, medical and financial interest. A good example is sea holly, growing on coastal sands and gravels, once extensive, but now rare from Walton to Dovercourt. The botantist John Gerard found plants growing near Landermere in the late 16th century and reports that the roots preserved in sugar 'nourish and restore the aged and amend the defects of nature in the younger'. He goes on to say that a goat with it in her mouth will stand still and the whole flock with her until the goatherd removes it from her. Culpepper in his 17th century herbal recommends it, amongst other things, as a cure for throat 'kernels'. This painful swelling of the lymph glands in the neck (scrofula) was once well known in this part of Essex. The common name, King's Evil, was used because of the belief that only the 'Royal Touch' could cure the affliction.

Edward the Confessor received the gift of touch-healing from God, it was believed, in the holy oil or chrism used at his coronation. Dr Samuel Johnson was the last person in England to receive the 'touch' from Queen Anne in 1712 when he was 9 months old. Charles II was reputed to have touched no less than 92,107 sufferers.

Any cure, other than the inconvenient appearing before a King or Queen, would therefore be popular and certainly easier to apply. The roots of sea holly were used from the 16th to 19th centuries as a cure for cramps, convulsions, falling sickness, liver problems and King's Evil. Crushed root was candied and sold as 'Eringoes' (from the Latin *Eryngium Maritimum*). As with so many plants the list of cures and beneficial properties grew. In the 16th century Eringoes were thought to be an aphrodisiac, mentioned by Falstaff in *The Merry Wives of Windsor.* The Latin name, incidentally, came originally from the Greek meaning a plant to cure indigestion or wind.

In the 1600s a certain Robert Buxton (or Burton) of Colchester made a concotion from the roots and marketed it under the name of 'Kissing Comfort', surely an early example of selling by association of ideas. The candied roots were a great speciality at Mayoral banquets in Colchester until the early 1900s. Collecting the plants from the shores of Hamford Water was a useful spare-time occupation and, as the roots were the saleable part, not surprisingly it is now very scarce. Considerable secrecy surrounded the recipe for candying the roots. When Buxton died in 1665 his apothecary apprentice, Samuel Great, continued manufacture, his family continuing until about 1797, when the last member, Christopher, died. This was not the end of the story because a maiden lady, Miss Thorn, who lived in the same parish, had the recipe and supplied Thomas Smith, a druggist of High Street, whenever he received an order for candied roots.

They ceased to be an article of commerce in Colchester about 1865, but Mrs Seamen (Miss Thorn's sister) gave the old recipe to Mr J C Shenstone, FLS, who recorded it for posterity:

> Roots must be dug up from a depth of at least 6 feet, then peeled and boiled until quite tender. Then soaked for several days in cold

Sea holly

Salsify

69

water, changing water occasionally. The pith is removed and the roots spread open with a bone mash. Then cut into very small strips and twisted to resemble barley sugar. Strips are then immersed in very strong syrup prepared from refined sugar with a little orange flower water, the syrup being boiled from time to time with fresh sugar. The strips are then dried in front of a fire on trays of plaited cane.

It is doubtful if anyone today would be prepared to face the herculean task of digging six feet in shingle for the roots of this interesting bluish green hairless plant on the shores of Hamford Water where at least one carefully guarded colony exists today. Whatever the reputed beneficial properties are they would not today warrant such a complicated recipe.

Gerard in 1597 gave a very similar recipe to the above, so manufacture of candied roots must have been fairly common and perhaps Colchester's Eringoe fame was because of the best roots and great skill in preparing them rather than to any secret recipe. The candied roots, Gerard said, 'Are exceeding good to be given unto old and aged people that are consumed and withered with age and which want naturall [sic] moisture. It is also good for other sorts of people that have no delight or appetite to venery'. Venery has two meanings – hunting and sexual indulgence: Robert Buxton, apothecary and manufacturer of Eringoes, probably exploited both.

A now rare plant of the shingle is the beautiful sea pea with purplish blue flowers, not unlike the modern garden sweet pea, except for variety of colour and lack of scent. It prefers fairly mobile shingle or light gravel and was found around Hamford Water in 1964 and 1970 and, hopefully, will come back if the handstrewn Suffolk seeds lovingly placed by conservationists manage to germinate and

Corn marigold

Corn cockle

flourish. Still common at Dunwich and other Suffolk shingle beaches, it was once a familiar sight in north east Essex. Like other leguminous plants it has the power to utilise atmospheric nitrogen directly to build proteins: cattle straying on to the shingle will eat it with relish. In times of famine or drought people of the coast were sometimes reduced to gathering the pods containing small mung sized peas to cook and eat, large quantities being needed to make a frugal meal.

What with cattle, people and disturbed beaches in the past hundred years the sea pea *(Lathyrus japonicus)* today has an extremely precarious hold in Hamford Water. However, as seeds are dispersed by the sea and can remain floating and viable for up to five years, some may turn up one day.

Another sad loss to the Sokens is the delightful 'Guilde Weed', against which Henry II issued an ordinance requiring the destruction of what had become a pernicious plant of cornfields in the 12th century. This beautiful golden flower, the corn marigold *(Chrysanthemum segetum)* survived attempts at eradication and was mentioned by Culpepper and by John Parkinson in *Theatrum Botannicum* in 1640. It continued to thrive until the 20th century being a 'troublesome weed' in corn, but modern farming has now all but destroyed it. In amateur field surveys of fields around Hamford Water every summer from 1984, no specimens have been found. The nearest colony found in 1986 was bordering a footpath through a cornfield in Levington, Suffolk. Unless agricultural methods change it may never be seen again in the Sokens.

Whether or not, as originally thought, it cured warts, promoted sweating, drove out smallpox and measles, helped cure jaundice and soothed sore eyes we may never know, but of one thing we can be sure, it brightened every cloudy day with golden glory.

Another plant to look out for on road sides and banks in Beaumont-cum-Moze and Oakley is salsify *(Tragopogon porrifolius)* for two reasons; one because it is handsome on a single stem with grass-like leaves and rich purple flower head and, secondly, because it was once grown by cottagers as a root vegetable and still occurs near sites of long gone dwellings as a useful hint to students of field archaeology. Before the flower head opens it looks rather like the yellow flowered goatsbeard.

It is difficult to find a plant which has increased in the area since Victorian days, however, one such is hog's fennel *(Peucedanum officinale)*. Gerard discovered it in Hamford Water in the 16th century; John Ray in mid-17th century; and George Stacey Gibson in the 19th century. Now it is plentiful (though nobody knows why) on and around Skippers Island and spreading along sea walls and even on roadsides in the Sokens. It occurs nowhere else in Essex, the only other site is at Faversham, Kent, in Gerard's 'medow neere to the seaside'.

A plant of the same family also called hog's fennel or milk parsley *(Peucedanum palustre)* is recorded in one site on the south coast, one in the south-west, several in Norfolk and a few in Lincolnshire. The name hog's fennel, common to both species, can thus be confusing to casual investigators. This point is important to note, because the Hamford Water and north Kent hog's fennel, *officinale,* or sulphur weed, is the sole home of a rare moth only recently identified as a distinct species, namely, *Gortyna Borelli,* Fisher's estuarine moth or Fisher's frosted orange. This moth, of approximately 2 inch width, takes wing in September: eggs are laid on the leaves, the caterpillars then eat their way down inside the stem and the chrysalis is formed in the stout woody root. How the ardent collectors of last century missed

73

such a large distinctive moth is puzzling: possibly emergence so late in the summer when school children were back at their desks and holidays were over for most people, reduced the chances of discovery.

Glaucium flavum, the yellow horned poppy is holding its own on a few gravelly beaches near Hamford Water. The seven localities for this essentially coastal plant noted by Gibson in mid 19th century are still producing, except Southend and Leigh, now completely developed and unsuitable. Once it was thought to be a remedy for bruises and thus named bruisewort: it would need to be a hefty bruise to persuade the injured to roam shingle at Stone Point, The Wade or Twizzle to obtain relief today: they would be fortunate to find one plant.

Wort is old English for plant and often one reputed to have healing characteristics would be named locally with the disease first and 'wort' as the suffix. Pewterwort is a good example of a country name relating to the useful purpose of a plant known as horsetail *(Equisetum arvense)*, abundant in the Sokens today. This primitive plant, resembling moth-eaten asparagus, without leaves, but with scaly sheaths at the joints, is largely ignored now, but was prized before the advent of silver-plated cutlery. The stems are hard and coated with silica and thus used of old for scouring copper pots and pans and particularly pewter, hence the name. Gradually, scouring with fine sand, followed by ashes, took its place, until Brasso emerged.

For centuries dried horsetail was sold by Colchester herbalists and apothecaries to make infusions for disordered bladders and inflammations and also to clear 'eruptions' (presumably boils). It is still sold in health shops as a comforting tea.

Another wort common in the Sokens is yarrow *(Achillea millefolium)* or, as once known, woundwort. The common name 'yarrow' survives from the Anglo-Saxon *gearwe* and is reputed to have been used by Achilles to staunch soldiers' wounds and was always included in army medical supplies as soldiers' woundwort or *herbe militaris.* Carpenters, joiners, sawyers and all woodworkers were also careful to have plants handy for cuts and gashes from chisels and saws, thus another common name was carpenters' grasse. In the *Grete Herball* of 1526 we learn 'it is good to rejoyn and soudre [unite] wounds'.

Truly can it be said that local and country names describe not only the reputed function of plants, but give us other insights into commonly held beliefs. An example is ground elder: introduced in the Middle Ages as a medicinal and pot-herb, it was, by Victorian times, a persistent weed hated by gardeners. Used externally as a fomentation it was thought to cure rheumatism, sciatica and gout: various names included goutwort and bishops'-weed. It speaks volumes for the popular view of bishops and their supposed bibulous affliction of gout that ground elder was named after them!

Owing to a relatively rugged independence of spirit born and bred into Kirby inhabitants by virtue of the Peculiar Jurisdiction of the Sokens they had enjoyed since the 10th century, whereby in day to day matters they were more subject to the Dean and Chapter of St Paul's, London, who had been granted (by King Athelstan and confirmed by King Cnut) the jurisdiction of Kirby, Thorpe and Walton, than they were to the Bishop of London, we can imagine Kirby gardeners consigning bishops'-weed and its trailing roots to the garden bonfire with relish. This enjoyment may well have been strengthened and spiced by the moral support of their illustrious vicar, William Burgess (1823), who, being well versed in legal matters, defended the rights of the Sokens to such good effect that the Bishop of London had on one occasion to write a conciliatory letter to him, virtually apologising for usurping his powers.

Hog's fennel

Chapter Seven

Oysters - John Smith - Oyster spawning - Oyster enemies - Oyster glossary

Although Hamford oysters have never reached worldwide fame as have 'native' Essex oysters from the Colchester Fishery in Pyefleet (separating Mersea Island from Langenhoe Marshes), they have been eaten at least since Roman times and almost certainly well before that. It has to be admitted that their quality is slightly inferior to the 'native', mainly due to the muddy bottom of Hamford Water and the relatively little husbandry received when compared with the meticulous cultivation through the centuries in Pyefleet and other rivers and creeks between South Foreland and Orford Ness.

However, before the days of large sewage outfalls from the Harwich area, Hamford Water was cleaner and the oysters therefore better. The Romans, on their excellent roads and with their leadlined wooden water tanks, transported live Essex oysters (including those from Hamford, probably landed at Beaumont Quay) throughout Britain; nearly all Roman sites contain dumps of oyster shells and Essex shells have been identified in Rome itself.

Incidentally Tacitus and Caesar optimistically referred to pearls as an extractive industry of value from Britain. Whether oysters were an added incentive in Caesar's decision to invade Britain, an unattributed poem printed in a 1920 guide book to Clacton, Walton, Frinton and Colchester is intriguing as poetical confirmation of their importance to the Roman palate –

The old luxurious Romans vaunt did make
Of lustful oysters, took in Lucrine Lake.
Your Essex better hath, and such perchance
As tempted Caesar first to pass from France.

We do not know how disappointed the Romans were when they found that cold water oysters from Essex, unlike tropical oysters, do not produce precious pearls. No doubt the quest was an excuse to eat more in the hope of finding treasure!

The earliest Charter for oyster fishing was granted to Colchester in 1189 during the reign of Richard I and confirmed the *then existing* rights with regard to the Fishery, so the Charter merely confirmed an anciently exercised and well established trade. Fishing rights elsewhere were sometimes licensed by the Lord of the Manor. Poaching on the Lord's oyster beds of Landermere was so active in 1674 that a penalty of £20 for each offence was prescribed: apparently this was not sufficient deterrent as the penalty was increased to £40 within two years. It seems that no one was caught until 1678 when the bailiff was ordered to levy much reduced sums from strangers and vagrants who had taken oysters out of Hamford Water without the Lord's license in the unseasonable months of May, June and July. Four Brightlingsea men were fined £5 each, as were two from Harwich.

Other large areas of the Essex coast have for many years contained 'common ground' where anyone could dredge for oysters or oyster spat; the spat and young oysters (brood) could then be sold to the proprietors of oyster layings in the estuaries: Hamford Water was no exception.

In January, 1882, when vigorous exception was taken to the prospect of granting oyster and mussel fishing rights to John Smith of Burnham, one point was made that 'these waters are now and ever have been purely and entirely free public and common waters for fishing, navigation and all marine uses'. The Colne Fishery Company also objected to John Smith's application because 'dredgermen in their right as part of the General Public have long fished for floating fish, oyster spat and young oysters in these waters'. That company regularly bought young oysters for fattening from Hamford fishermen and probably feared that John Smith would supply competitors as well, restricting their own suppliers in their dredging. The row continued for 4 months.

A Local Government Board of Inquiry met at the Marine Hotel, Walton, on 11th April, 1882, to consider the matter, with the Board inspector Mr E Thurston Holland in charge of the lengthy meeting. This was eventually adjourned and another held on 19th April, also lengthy and indeterminate. It was finally agreed to adjourn once again until the Inspector had had time to inspect the backwaters himself. The next meeting was not reported by the *Walton & Clacton Gazette,* but on Wednesday, 26th July, 1882, they printed a short paragraph to the effect that Mr John Smith obtained permission to fish for oysters and mussels in Hamford Water, but was not to interfere with other forms of fishing. In the event, he never exercised the permission granted; probably several factors contributed to this failure to exploit such an apparently valuable concession. First, local hostility must have been uncomfortable, to say the least; second, Essex oyster farming companies may well have been reluctant to change their regular suppliers of young oysters; and thirdly and probably the most important, it may have been the vast and expensive beds of culch (clean empty shells) needed to be strewn in Hamford Water on which to breed oysters in marketable quantities. Mr Smith may have found out quickly that he had bitten off more than he could chew.

Oysters were (and still are) very big business in Essex. For example, some idea of the proliferation of Essex oysters and the size of the industry can be gained from the report that in 1895 over two and a half million Colchester Pyefleet oysters were sold for £20,000.

Wild oysters have survived in Hamford Water for centuries, but to provide first class readily marketable molluscs, complicated and expensive husbandry is required, as is a knowledge of their life cycle. The British oyster *(Ostrea edulis)* thrives best in unpolluted water covering beds of London clay, hence the fame of Essex oysters. Oysters have no sex life in that copulation is not needed for propogation and there is a variation of sex in each oyster at different periods in the breeding season.

During the spatting (spawning) season, the oyster discharges spawn into the water, to float freely until drawn into the gills of other oysters, thus making contact with and fertilising eggs attached to the gills: at this stage the oystermen refer to them as 'white sick'. After a time these white eggs develop extremely small hard black shells - miniscule oysters, in fact. Such 'pregnant' oysters are called 'black sick'. By rapid closing of the shell the young are discharged into the water like a puff of smoke. These tiny oysters (spat) rise to the surface to be carried about by tide and current, eventually to sink to the bottom.

As each oyster discharges a million or two, and as the sea bed is not carpeted with oysters, the mortality is clearly very great. At this stage there are many predators and hazards, frost being particularly deadly. Survivors then have to find by chance a clean shell or hard surface of the sea bed on which to adhere and grow. For the next two or three years of growing in a fixed position on culch (shells) they are known as 'brood' oysters. Commercial oyster fishermen assist this settling down of young oysters by spreading clean shells over the beds of London clay to give a safe nursery for the brood. Such labour and expense may have daunted John Smith as his permission was granted, provided he did not interfere with existing fishing; unfortunately for him, this had for centuries included dredging for oysters and oyster spat and he may have realised that any improvements he made to encourage breeding would also help the locals.

Of many hazards confronting oysters, water pollution, the obvious danger, will not, unless very severe, kill the oysters, but may well kill those who eat them!

Before the spat have attached themselves to culch on the bottom they are often eaten by fish and shrimps and, even when anchored, can be 'hoovered off' by bottom feeding flatfish, which also abound in Hamford Water. The five finger starfish is also a very dangerous pest in an oyster fishery; it will clasp any it finds big enough to make into a useful meal and, inserting its stomach into the oyster, will digest the soft part *in situ.* A relative, the sea-hedgehog, *Echinus,* whose mouth is armed with five teeth, will scrape off any animal matter from the shells, including any spat settling there. The dog-whelk is another enemy capable of boring a hole through the shell, through which it inserts a sucker to absorb the body of the oyster. The common shore crab is also destructive with a strong claw to crush the smaller oysters and pick out the edible parts.

One of the most deadly predators is a

comparative new-comer, the slipper limpet was introduced by accident from America adhering to blue point oysters. This mollusc, rejoicing in the name *Crepidula fornicata,* is a formidable competitor for the same food as the oyster; it increases its numbers very fast, making huge clumps which smother the oysters; slimy secretions are deposited on the culch preventing young spat from settling; and mud and weed it attracts inhibits more legitimate settlers.

Alderman Laver, MD, Chairman of the Colne Fishery Board, in an erudite article entitled 'Colchester Oysters' published by *The Restaurant* magazine in November, 1911, reported that this pest arrived in the rivers and creeks north of the Thames about 1891 and was a 'most undesireable tenant' in their fishery. Whether or not John Smith of Burnham heard about this new threat we do not know, but if he did, no doubt he might even have welcomed this invasion as another justification for not taking up his oyster dredging license in Hamford Water.

As with any highly specialised industry there are many technical terms unique to oystermen, all of them ancient in use. The Essex and Suffolk words, adapted by dialect, are difficult to define etymologically, being both old and local and undoubtedly subject to pronunciation changes over many years -

NATIVE oysters: strictly speaking all oysters from South Foreland to Orford Ness can be called 'natives' and are bred on beds of London clay, but in common parlance the Colchester Pyefleet oysters, with the name a registered Trade Mark (vigorously defended from time to time in Courts of Law) are also referred to as 'natives'.

CULCH or, more correctly, CULTCH is described in the *Dialect Dictionary* as spawn of the oyster, but the local dredgermen use the term to describe empty shells thrown overboard on to the oyster grounds to which oyster spat will adhere.

SPAT is an interesting, imitative word, used by all oystermen for oyster spawn and also for young oysters up to the end of their first year. Probably derived from 'spit' as a description of the way the oyster ejects spawn by rapid closing of the shell.

BROOD describes young oysters from two to three years of age.

HALFWARE is the term for oysters from three to four years old, numbering about 1,600 to 1,800 to the tub or bushel

WARE or OYSTERS are marketable oysters requiring only a season on the fattening ground to reach full size, when approximately 1,200 will fill the tub or bushel.

Last century difficulties arose as to the exact size of the tubs or bushels in which oysters were conventionally sold and, at a meeting in Burnham in 1839, the matter was considered by all the principal oyster merchants of the district. In a short report it was stated that the old tubs contained 94 quarts, but it was agreed to make 92 quarts the standard in future. Presumably this still applies unless, of course, the Common Market has confused the matter recently!

Chapter Eight

Railways - Mistley, Thorpe & Walton - East Essex
Walton & Harwich Junction - Railway speculation
Traffic - Parkeston Quay - Harwich business - Krakatoa

This century we have seen the North Sea oil bonanza and marvelled at such enormous engineering achievements. Vast reservoirs of finance and expertise, as well as oil and gas, have been tapped with significant results for the benefit of the whole country. It may be wondered whether the past had anything as ambitious and profitable: in fact, the great railway boom from the mid 19th century until the Great War was, in many ways, comparable.

Tangible results of this railway boom and fever can be illustrated by a brief survey of the rapid building of railways in east Essex. Vast sums of money were forthcoming for what seemed certain profits. It was thought that nothing could stem the flood of progress and, despite the constraints of pick, shovel, wheelbarrow and horse and cart, ambitious engineering projects involving tunnels, bridges, viaducts and cuttings were undertaken with courage and ingenuity. Objections from landowners reluctant to lose their land or vistas of tranquility were overcome. Compulsory purchase powers, now more familiar, came into their own, largely as a result of railway building backed by Act of Parliament, not only in Essex, but nationwide.

84

Some idea of the incredible speed of development can be gathered from the opening dates of railways in or leading to Tendring Hundred –

29 March, 1843	Brentwood to Colchester
15 June, 1846	Colchester to Ipswich (via Manningtree)
2 July, 1849	Colchester to Hythe
15 August, 1854	Manningtree to Harwich
8 May, 1863	Hythe to Wivenhoe
8 January, 1866	Wivenhoe to Weeley
18 April, 1866	Wivenhoe to Brightlingsea
28 July, 1866	Weeley to Kirby Cross
17 May, 1867	Kirby Cross to Walton
4 July, 1882	Thorpe le Soken to Clacton
29 August, 1882	A spur from the Colchester Ipswich line to Mistley

Every sod of earth for these works had to be lifted and moved by the hands of vast armies of navvies (often Irish), using manual tools and equipment developed generations before the steam age.

Estates in the ownership of the same families for centuries were chopped in half and buildings were demolished or obstructed, all in the name of progress and profit. Fortunes were made – and sometimes lost. Inevitably there was some skullduggery, the railway companies themselves not being immune. A practice by no means unknown was for an incognito railway nominee or agent to buy land before publication of a proposed railway development to avoid the company having to pay the customary 10% extra paid under compulsory purchase. Private individuals 'in the know' were not above doing the same as a gamble.

In the late 1890s a possibly significant and definitely comprehensive sale of land and property occurred in Walton. Whole rows of cottages and land were included and one wonders whether the proposed railway extension from Walton to Harwich was the underlying reason for this, especially as some of the purchasers were also involved in the never-to-be—railway. More of this failed project later.

One could be forgiven for thinking that building and running railways was as good as printing money, but there were the usual hazards, which have a familiar ring. A half yearly report of the Great Eastern Railway in 1886 gives a hint of this, when the directors told the shareholders that receipts for goods traffic were reduced because of the diminished quantity of grain carried by rail and the partial failure of herring fishing: poor grain harvests were recorded in Tendring in 1877, 1879, 1882, 1883 and 1885, being described as below average or deficient. Nevertheless the entrepreneurs were not to be put off.

Two remarkable abortive schemes indicative of over-optimism and what we would call defective market research are worthy of note. The first was begun in 1864 and abandoned in 1869, but despite this disaster another scheme, only a few miles away, was under discussion and negotiation as soon after as 1881, only to be abandoned shortly afterwards, regardless of the elaborate and costly plans, sections and a Parliamentary Bill deposited in 1882.

Work on the first actually began and relics remain to this day. It was the ill-fated Mistley, Thorpe & Walton Railway, ably recorded, written up and privately published by Thos. B Peacock of Halstead in 1946. Later, interest was revived by reporter Lesley Pallet in an article in the *Harwich & Manningtree Standard* in 1960. The ambitious proposal was to link the rapidly developing 19th century coastal resort of Walton on the Naze with Ipswich via the Great Eastern Railway. The Tendring Hundred Railway from Colchester to Walton was to take the anticipated traffic from the south via Colchester. Exactly what were the full ambitions behind this project are not recorded or have not yet come to light, but we do know that paddle steamers packed with trippers plied the coast between piers and 'ozone' (healthy breezes) from the sea was a new fad assiduously sought after by those with the railway or steamer fare to hand. Salt water bathing was also popular and beaches capable of taking discrete bathing machines on wheels were earmarked for exploitation. The gently sloping beaches of Clacton and Walton were developed and well advertised: Frinton followed at the turn of the century.

Travel agents had not yet come into their own, but railway companies, town councils and steamer companies pursued vigorous advertising campaigns to great effect. So, work began after Notice of the Bill for the railway was deposited on 12 November, 1862. The line was to start at a point east of Mistley station, passing through Bradfield, Wix, Little Bentley, Tendring, Weeley, Beaumont-cum-Moze, Thorpe-le-Soken, Kirby-le-Soken, Great Holland and Frinton, ending in a field to the west of Walton churchyard. The railway was incorporated by an Act dated 21 July, 1863, with authorised capital of £60,000 and £20,000 on loan.

Compulsory purchase of the necessary land was to take place within two years, while five years was allowed to complete the works. The Great Eastern Railway was authorised to subscribe £20,000, to appoint two directors and to work the line at 48% of the receipts – not a bad yield, but never realised. A proposal was made and approved that the recently incorporated Tendring Hundred Railway from Colchester, north to Wivenhoe (opened in March, 1863), would join the proposed line to Thorpe-le-Soken. The additional Act was sanctioned by the 1864 Mistley, Thorpe & Walton Railway Act.

The great day for turning the first sod was 6 April, 1864, and was a glittering occasion full of the

Victorian sense of showmanship and protocol. Everyone knew and observed their place in the social strata at the ceremonies and enjoyed the experience of welcoming special London trains full of contractors, friends, directors, shareholders and families, all ready to cheer the Colchester Volunteer Band of welcome. Specially planted commemorative fir trees in station yard and roadway were duly admired by all.

The Rector of Little Oakley, Rev. George Burmester, unknowingly prophesied in his opening prayer for the future, "We thank thee, O Lord, for warning us in Thy Sacred Word against the greediness of filthy lucre. Grant, we beseech Thee, that the transactions of this day may not result in so sad an end". Less than twelve months later a bitter dispute arose, culminating in the abandonment of the whole project and with a certain amount of physical violence sealing its fate, as well as fulfilling the rector's apprehensions.

What happened was sad, but typical of so many ambitious projects. The Mistley, Thorpe & Walton Railway Company's engineer, James Cooke, complained vigorously that the contractor, William Munro, was making only slow progress, so he assigned the contract to Frederick Furness. Munro had explained in excuse that he only received possession of the land towards the end of the period agreed for completion and also he had been prevented from using the land by an expediently named Mr Mustard of Tendring Green, who had formally [i.e. physically] ejected the workmen from the land under development. To make matters worse and the temperature hotter, James Cooke then suggested there was a nought too many in the account for £2,000 presented by Munro.

A vicious and bloody battle was fought between 50 navvies commanded by Munro's agent and about 60 longshoremen and lumpers from Harwich, tougher, as it turned out, than the navvies who retired to lick their wounds and bruises.

The half yearly meeting was told on 30 August, 1865, in a tense and apprehensive atmosphere, that £26,391.12.11d had already been spent, but it was hoped that work on the Tendring to Thorpe section would be finished by the spring. Unfortunately and inevitably, public confidence in the Mistley project had been undermined mortally by this time and, with the Company's debt to the contractor standing at £12,000, work was abruptly stopped. On 8 July, 1869, at a private shareholders' meeting, it was resolved to apply to the Board of Trade to abandon the railway and this was speedily done the next month.

The unfortunate contractor held an auction sale of the equipment and goods at the Thorn Hotel, Mistley, raising a miserable £2,000. Next came the sale of the land: a detailed assessment of land values carried out by the parish overseers of Tendring, Wix and Beaumont amounted to only £22.5.0d. for just under 36 acres, six further acres in the cuttings being deemed worthless.

The death throes included one last convulsive jerk of the dying body with a hope that the railway line would still be built after all if a proposed new East Essex Railway Company could be formed by resuscitating the Mistley, Thorpe & Walton Railway, but this came to nothing. All has slept since.

Some indication of the increasingly desperate attempts at completion can be seen from three changes of plan. The first was to link Mistley with Walton via Tendring and Kirby-le-Soken; the second modified this by suggesting a link from Tendring to Thorpe-le-Soken, thus using the existing Colchester to Walton line; the third, and most forlorn, was to build a link from Tendring to Weeley.

Apart from deposited plans and various records

Mistley/Harwich Road Bridge over the never-built railway

in local newspaper archives all that remains today are the arched brick bridge carrying the Mistley to Harwich road over the abandoned railway; Arch Cottage, Wix, near traces of brick footings of the proposed railway arch; signs of a cutting and embankment intended to conduct the road over the line at Tendring Heath (widened for military purposes in 1940, but never needed to impede any invasion of tanks during World War II); and remains of a railway arch to carry the track over the site of a road at Tendring. In 1946 part of this arch was being used as a stable. For those interested in failed enterprises from the heyday of Victorian progresss these partly constructed relics can still be found in neglected isolation.

The second fiasco is, in many ways, more intriguing as, despite the existing and extensive preparatory details, no work on the land was even begun to connect Walton with Harwich by bridging the eastern end of Hamford Water. Had both these railway schemes come to fruition the Soken territory would have been completely encircled by railway lines.

From the existing deposited plans no hint can be gleaned of the motives initiating the idea, but probably the national euphoria generated by providing any sort of railway and the conviction that progress for a district lay in that provision, while if those propagating the scheme were men of note and what was then called 'the quality', any hare-brained enterprise, however over-optimistic, would warrant and receive some support.

Even today, with only local pleasure craft and a few small fishing vessels using the approaches to Hamford Water, any suggestion of a railway bridge restricting entry to the backwaters would be stifled at birth, but in 1881 with many fishing smacks and sailing barges, in addition to private boating, using the backwaters far more extensively, the idea still gained credence, incredible as it might seem. Unravelling the story of the railway-that-never-was between Harwich and Walton across the water began when local historians unearthed a comprehensive set of plans in the Council House, Old Road, Frinton.

A bound multi-paged large scale map was found, entitled 'Walton & Harwich Junction Railway' and marked 'In Parliamentary Session 1881/1882', together with an eight page book of reference. The map was produced by William Dennis and Alex Thuey, engineers, with Phillip Brannon as architect. The reference book was compiled by Edward Chapman, Lord of the Manor, Harwich, and E F Harvey, Surveyor of Highways. Solicitors were Cooke & Partners of Chancery Lane, the Parliamentary Agent being William Bell of Great George Street, Westminster. So far research has not located any successors of the above nor have the Law Society been able to pinpoint the solicitors. In any case 25 years is the maximum length of time that solicitors normally hold records. Chancery Lane itself has been the subject of large-scale rebuilding and early addresses are no longer relevant. Motives for the Walton to Harwich railway cannot be ascertained from the original sources.

What is known from the map is that this ambitious rail link was to be built north of Walton station and the Parish Church, at the junction of Kirby Road with Walton High Street, going over Sole Creek and Warner's Dock alongside Walton back waters, then over Cormorant Creek to seaward of the sea wall, leaving the mainland at Stone Point and across the water to the parish of Great Oakley, crossing Dugmore Creek near Cutter's Hard, then south of Foulton Hall, curving down to Dovercourt over Ramsey Creek and finally joining the Great Eastern Railway line, Harwich branch, at Dock

Bridge.

Even the most casual stroller walking from Walton backwaters through the Naze to Stone Point will marvel at the intrepid engineers prepared to undertake such a task on extremely difficult terrain.

The reference book contains a comprehensive list of all properties, owners, lessees and occupiers along the proposed route. No record of any purchase of the necessary land has yet come to light, but local newspapers of the late 19th century do give interesting insights to the considerable degree of progress made, at least, with the public relations angle and as time went by with no work begun, the sales promotion, which itself led to reporting adverse factors of trade, before complete silence fell on the idea.

Motives and reasons behind such a scheme are fascinating, but difficult to determine from records. The Victorians, perhaps because minutes of meetings were written laboriously in longhand and therefore of necessity kept short, were pastmasters at producing minutes of meetings containing only the barest facts of decisions taken as a result of largely unrecorded discussion and debate. It is necessary, therefore, to try to read between the lines and use conjecture to arrive at any conclusion.

That the scheme was seriously entertained can be deduced from the fact that the famous Peter Bruff was involved. The proven history of his improvement achievements in north east Essex, particularly in Clacton, Walton and Harwich are sufficient testimonials to his ability. His heavy involvement can be seen from an article in the *Gazette* for Wednesday, 18 January, 1882, reporting a quarterly meeting of the Harwich Harbour Conservancy Board at Holborn Viaduct Hotel, London, on 12 January. Engineer Peter Bruff's report was read out, including a paragraph on the Walton & Harwich

Junction Railway. The intriguing heading for this article was 'The Felixstowe Dock, Harwich & Walton Railway'. One may well wonder why Felixstowe Dock was included.

The relevant section of his report reads –

This project for which plans, sections and a Bill have been deposited, affects your jurisdiction at the same part as the proposed Fishery Order, although in a much more serious manner, inasmuch as it is proposed to cross the entrance to such waters 10 feet above high tide by bridging for 1,000 yards of varying fixed openings, those in the main navigable channel itself being mostly of 100 feet span; with a single movable opening near the centre of 50 feet span, for it is presumed the passage of shipping having fixed masts. No explanations however are given by the plans or in the Bill how such fixed openings are to be constructed or movable opening regulated, or position of the whole bridging to be indicated during night or in foggy weather, which seem important to have provided for, as well as suitable seaward defence works, to guard against partially unmanageable craft being driven by storm against the fixed instead of through the opening part of the work, thereby possibly receiving and doing great damage, which latter event would not be unlikely to happen whenever vessels cast ashore on the Pye Sand hold together long enough to beat into it into the deep-water channel and thence into the waters in question, of which there are wellknown instances.

Peter Bruff then added a footnote saying that 50 feet was narrow for a seaway and it would be better with 2 at 75 feet balanced on a central pier.

After the report was delivered verbally, the Chairman, Colonel Tomline, said, "We see no objection to it". The Engineer replied, "Not the slightest". The report was ordered to be sent to the Board of Trade.

The inclusion of Felixstowe in the local newspaper heading, thus associating these new docks with Harwich and Walton, may simply have been because this was a meeting of the Harwich Harbour Board, who were responsible for the whole of the confluence of the rivers Stour and Orwell and thus for the Felixstowe side of the water. Even then Felixstowe was growing rapidly as a port and, within a year, the opening of Parkeston Quay was to be announced. Harwich may well have been having jitters about competition and were anxious to shew that, because of a venerable maritime history, they were still to be reckoned with and could still, if necessary, contemplate building a rail link across the water to Felixstowe, which, after all, was only fractionally wider than the proposed Hamford Water bridge span.

Whatever the motives were, they must have been powerful and compelling, as this was a sensitive area in view of fishing interests and ancient rights and, particularly with the four-year-old memory of the forcible objections raised by scores of influential people at John Smith's request for permission to fish Hamford Water for oysters and mussels. The motives for building the bridge were also strong enough to overcome the private interests of the architect of the scheme, Phillip Brannon, who was a lessee of Sir John H Johnson of lands and foreshore abutting the sea in Hamford Water and had personally and vigorously objected to the 'cruel injustice' of fishing rights being assigned to anyone else, especially as the locals had enjoyed

such rights since 'time immemorial'. He must therefore have been sensitive to any suggestion disturbing
the *status quo* of these waters. It is puzzling that
he was still apparently quite happy to be the
architect of a scheme that would result in a railway
bridge virtually sealing off such lucrative and
productive waters or, at least, restricting their
convenient usage. It was also on his doorstep!

We shall never know all the ramifications
behind Victorian aspirations for linking Walton to
Harwich by rail, but we do know something of the
impulsive railway mania of the day. Dozens of newspapers, assuming railway titles, were begun nationwide, often containing 16 to 24 extra pages of
advertisements concerning possible or impossible
schemes, all vaunted optimistically. The general
theme was that a railway link meant prosperity and
profit. Consequently, thousands of investors backed
their conditioned aspirations with hard cash or
promises of the same.

Ominous signs that all was not necessarily
always well with railway finances appear to have
been ignored in the euphoria of progress. Signs began
to be manifest in the reports from newspapers. The
Harwich & Dovercourt Free Press on 7 February,
1885, reported the 45th half yearly General Meeting
of the Great Eastern Railway as mentioning a
decrease in 1st and 2nd class traffic, also on
merchandise traffic suffering a 'grievous loss' on the
non-movement of grain, particularly wheat: the low
prices of wheat having induced farmers to hold
stocks and to use them for feeding purposes. It was
pointed out that the railway lost, not only the
carriage of wheat, but also the conveyance of oil
cakes. They were glad to be able to report an
increase in the sale of season tickets as a palliative
to shareholders. The local editorials gave no hint,
however, that depressing commercial traffic news

had any bearing on the proposed railway.

At this stage the boom mentality seems to have survived such set-backs and it can easily be imagined that an industrialised nation who, even last century, seriously contemplated a Channel Tunnel, would feel that problems and minor hiccups in railway building were simply challenges to ingenuity and technology. After all, in the Commons had not Mr Chamberlain in April, 1883, moved that a committee of five members be appointed to join with a committee of the House of Lords to enquire whether it was expedient that Parliamentary sanction should be given to a submarine (i.e. tunnel) communication between England and France! In June, 1883, they even discussed in committee the danger of hostile explosions being used to obstruct such a tunnel. Walton to Harwich by rail across Hamford Water would seem very small beer in such times.

Another motive can be deduced from the reflection of certain public opinions and fears expressed in editorials in the local papers. Harwich residents had viewed the development and inevitable competition coming from Parkeston Quay with apprehension. The local paper on 17 March, 1883, carried the following comment

> Parkeston is now open to the general public and station and pier alive now with employees of the Great Eastern Railway Co... No expense has been spared, every thing being executed in the most elaborate style... We understand that cheap dinners for those employed by the Company are to be served at Parkeston... What a contrast with the now deserted Continental pier at Harwich where all was bustle and life now nothing but quietness reigns supreme... We do not wish it to be thought that we are under the impression that trade will leave

us all at once, but go it must, sooner or later, and Harwich will have to return to the days when the grass was growing green in the streets that was previous to the opening of the Great Eastern Railway, unless some enterprising individual or company will come forward and develop new resources of trade for the Borough.

The local reporters and editor would know of the proposed rail link and it is reasonable to suggest they were giving a preparatory plug for the development and the enterprising local individuals behind the scheme.

To shew that Harwich was still very much alive they were no doubt delighted to be able to report in April, 1883, that 'large consignments of mussels were shipped to Rotterdam by Harwich and Brightlingsea fishing smacks by order of the Dutch government for stocking their rivers'. Having reported that railway receipts were down, mainly though the corn trade recession, it was satisfying to report that mussels were doing well.

Rumours that some of the disastrous harvests, causing reduced rail traffic, were because of volcanic eruptions and not by any failure of private enterprise were fanned discretely by regular reporting of the Java catastrophe. In September, 1883, details of a telegram received by the Admiralty from Commander William Collins of HMS *Swift,* 9 September, were reported by the *Harwich & Dovercourt Free Press* in full, as follows

Arrived Batavia yesterday, leave today Sunda Straights. Great Channel probably unchanged. Much floating pumice. Channels between Krakatoa and Sebooko blocked. Anjer light extinct. Admiral (Dutch) informs me his ships will cruise in entrance to Straits for 3 months warning vessels.

The Victorians' philosophy enabled them to live more comfortably with disasters brought about by Acts of God than by human failures in the great entrepreneurial drives of the times. After all, no one could do anything about the first, but enterprise and hard work could overcome the latter throughout the Empire, as demonstrably it often did and had.

Apparently the Walton-Harwich link had not yet been assigned to the shelf and railway fever was further stimulated under 'local news' by an editorial reporting, 'It is stated a line has been projected for better communication between Birmingham and Harwich by way of Marks Tey, Coggeshall, Bishop's Stortford and Hitchin, using the present line between Braintree and Bishop's Stortford'. As the editorial carefully avoids saying by whom the above was stated it could have been a local attempt to boost the importance of Harwich by reporting hearsay.

From a research of local newspapers of the last decade of the 19th century, a blanket of silence appears to fall on the plans to bridge Walton with Harwich across the water. Even the meticulously kept minute books of the Harwich Harbour Conservancy Board for the years 1879 to 1905 failed to provide further concrete information on the illfated proposal. Complete silence reigned over the publications of the whole district from 1883.

How and why this scheme ground to a halt remains a matter of conjecture. Probably the ghostly spectre of the failed Mistley, Thorpe & Walton Railway hovered in the boardroom shadows; declining goods traffic figures on the balance sheets acted as cautionary factors; the development of Felixstowe Dock and Parkeston Quay proved to be a competitive distraction; and, possibly above all, the poor health of one of the most dynamic men in the area connected with this and other projects may have left the entrepreneurial driving seat empty or only filled by a learner driver.

The swish of the final curtain might well be heard in the businesslike minute recorded on 12 June, 1895, by the Harwich Harbour Board – 'In view of Mr Bruff's state of health the General Purposes Committee suggested he be invited to accept the position of Consulting Engineer at the nominal salary of 50 guineas per annum'. The clerk's salary for full time work had been only £90 a year in 1884.

Thomas Miller was appointed as Acting Engineer in place of Mr Bruff on 18 June, 1895, at 60 guineas a year salary – his full time services were valued at just 10 guineas more than the consultant's honorary fee. Perhaps he truncated the work load to match the reduced fee and thus the ambitious railway died on a dusty shelf.

So the unique sea inlet of Hamford Water remains to this day without encirclement by railway lines.

Lower Street, Kirby-le-Soken, c.1900.

101

Chapter Nine

Mrs Alice Jackson's memories - School - Wages -
Trippers - Camp meetings - World War II

Mrs Alice Jackson, writing her (unpublished) memoirs in 1964 described life in Kirby-le-Soken as she remembered it as a child. We gain a graphic picture of tranquillity and peace with glimpses of the contentment villagers enjoyed in such a close-knit community, despite hardships endured.

She was born at the turn of the century in a cottage opposite the church in a block known as Workhouse Cottages, built, she says, in the shape of a horseshoe. She calls Kirby-le-Soken Lower Kirby at the end of the Halstead Road, pronounced in her day 'Hosstead'. She records that several cottages were 'boarded' with no front gardens, but with plenty of ground at the rear and recalls nearly 40 that have been pulled down since her childhood. Her delight on the way home from school was to watch the blacksmith shoeing horses (the smith's shop is now a petrol filling station) or, better still, to call at the slaughter house to witness pigs and sheep being killed and prepared for the butcher's.

Transport was 'Shank's pony' or 'a ride in the carrier's cart to Thorpe or Colchester'. She continues "I've heard my father say he used to walk to Clacton many a time and I remember his first bicycle with hard rubber tyres needing no pumping."

The inhabitants "were mostly related to one another, it was either your aunt or first or second cousin who lived up the Street. There were so many with the same Christian, as well as Surname, they had to have a nickname. I think there must have been a lot of children in the village... in a magazine extract of 1887 there were 110 children at a Sunday School treat, this was usually a ride in a farm wagon to Walton... one wonders how these small cottages held such large families... but I suppose this was overcome by putting up a blanket as a partition in the bedrooms and having meals in relays".

Mrs Jackson was one of nine children and, although her parents had a hard time in making ends meet, she reports she never went to bed hungry. "Our chief meal was suet pudding and moist brown sugar to fill us before the vegetable course, meat was out of the question, apart from a small portion on Saturday or Sunday. When I was sent to buy the weekend joint, it was to be no more than half a crown. The midday meal of sandwiches were taken to be eaten at school as this was $1\frac{1}{2}$ mile walk. At 13 years old we were allowed to leave school, providing we could produce a Certificate to say we had a situation to go to, so we were fitted out with our Print Dresses, Caps, Aprons, and some sets of Unbleached Calico Underwear, all put in a small tin trunk, and with our Hair Style in a little bun, we were soon transformed into little old women to fend for ourselves. My first situation was 5 miles away and this I had to walk on my afternoon out, needless to say I got homesick... two and sixpence weekly was the wage to start with and by the time I was married it was fifteen shillings. The Homes were lit by Oil Lamp, one wonders how more fires did not occur, but you seldom heard of one overturning. One memory I shall always treasure...

L to R: Post Office (pulled down 1925); Royal Oak & Mrs Woolard; small Chapel of Rest; Butcher's shop. 1905

was Sunday afternoon in the front room, a treat in the Winter time when my father used to get out his accordion and play various tunes from Sankey & Moodey hymns and get the children to sing. I had a very happy childhood and trust that my seven Children will be able to say the same when they recall memories. My family has been in the Village for Generations according to the Tombstones in the Churchyard. My Grandparents kept the Royal Oak Public House, this is now known as Street House. The Grandfather was the Village Undertaker and his four sons acted as Bearers. It was at the Beerhouse where the mothers who had their Babies vaccinated at the Post Office adjoining were each given a penny to get a half pint of Porter... Life was lived very simply in the early 1900s, no kind of entertainment, just an occasional Magic Lantern Show at the Church Hall, a yearly fair held on the Ship Meadow, and a walk to Walton when the Circus was there, usually held on Bathhouse Meadow and it was a big thrill when the Hurdy Gurdy man came round, also the man with the Performing Bear.

"In the summer months, Brake loads of Trippers would drive through from Walton, and the children used to run behind chanting a Rhyme until a few coppers were thrown out to them. Money was scarce then and as soon as the Boys of the Village reached the age of 10 or 11 they used to trudge to Frinton to the Golf Links to carry Golf Clubs for the Gentlemen and Lady Players and used to come home very footsore and weary and the two and six-pence earned went towards buying some new clothes. Many of the women too used to walk to Frinton as Charwomen to earn half a crown working from 9 until 4 or others would take in huge Baskets of Laundry, which were collected and delivered for a few pence by a man who owned a horse and cart.

"Another memory is the Camp Meetings, a

kind of United Open Air Service, held on Mr Bevan's Meadow, then known as The Park, and a Big Attraction was the Great Holland and Kirby Brass Band to accompany the singing of Hymns, also the Chapel Anniversary held once a year in the School, as the little corrugated iron Methodist Chapel was too small to hold the amount of people who attended. This occasion usually meant a new hat or dress, incidentally the Chapel still stands, and until recently was used as a Storehouse by a Nurseryman. I suppose we are fortunate in having such a beautiful Church in the Village and it holds many Happy Memories for me myself and four sisters married there also five of my own children married there too..."

For a time Mrs Jackson was the church verger and recalls how she had to unlock the church door for services and, on one occasion, in deep snow. She mentions that village sanitation was primitive, but that mains water was introduced in 1930; previously the water system comprised seven wayside taps of good spring water given to the village by Squire Blanchard to save them having to buy water from a watercart at one penny a bucket.

She continues: "At one time a titled Lady lived at Kirby Hall and the Boys were taught to doff their caps and Girls to curtsy if her Ladyship passed in her carriage, on another occasion there was a very Grand Wedding being held at Brick Barn and all the villagers were invited to see the display of Wedding Presents on view. Life in the country is very nice, we had our own Game for whatever Season there was, such as Fivestones, Hopscotch, Hoop Bowling, Marbles or Skipping, not quite such hectic Games as played by the present Generation".

She compares the numerous village activities and organisations in 1960 towards the close of her life, and the huge increase in traffic to the coast.

She remembers three poplar trees being planted to commemorate King George V's Coronation... "I understand that years ago a fair used to be held on this same stretch of Green. Before Kirby was taken over by Frinton & Walton Council it came under the Tendring Hundred Parish Council. Caravan sites have sprung up which takes away the whole atmosphere of what was once a sleepy little village, yet the charm still remains, and some of its old houses dating back three and four hundred years. When the War Memorial was moved from the Bottom of Halstead Road to its present site the old foundations of a Cage were found which was used years ago to lock up any undesirable characters, hence the name Cage Corner, which is still called that by older inhabitants. During the Second World War our Children of the village were excavicated [*sic*] from the Coast to safer parts of the Country, altho' we had no Air Attacks here, apart from a few broken windows and one man killed right at the extreme end of the village by a Flying Bomb, this turned out to be a very safe zone. Now several of the New Bungalows are being occupied by retired couples, for the peace and quiet of the Countryside, taking pride in their gardens and enjoying their leisure hours surrounded by the Green Fields and Trees. Having lived in my house for over 45 years, I think I can at least say I've taken root now and hope to remain in my Home Town to the end of my time and I trust that whoever follows on will be as happy as I've been".

Bless her heart, her hope was fulfilled and she died in 1978, rich in memories and contentment, and was laid to rest in her beloved soil of Lower Kirby in the ancient Sokens.

What more can be said? – May God bless her contented soul.

ACKNOWLEDGMENTS

For invaluable help with documents, photographs and local knowledge, both general and specific, my grateful thanks to

Hervey Benham, Esq.
Lt.Col. G W Hawkes
J B Fisher, Esq.
Miss Irene J Johnson
Sebastian Dalrymple, Esq.
J V C Clarke, Esq.
Mrs Jane Bedford
Mrs Wendy Ibbotson
Mrs Rosalie E Smith
Mrs I M Humphreys
Mrs Lesley Pallett
A F Foster, Esq.
Mrs A P Smith
Mrs J Patricia Ford
Mrs Joy Lilley
I A Headley, Esq.
E J Cressey, Esq.
Messrs F T Everard & Sons, Ltd.
Messrs Crescent Shipping, Ltd.
Harwich Harbour Board
Frinton & Walton Gazette and Harwich & Manningtree Standard for access to their archives
Staff at the Record Offices in Colchester and Chelmsford
Staff at the Reference Library, Colchester
Members of the University of Cambridge Extra Mural Group at Thorpe-le-Soken, and especially the Secretary, Mrs D Ronson
And to many residents in the Tendring Hundred Peninsular for their willing sharing of local knowledge and legend.

For factual errors and faulty conclusions I take full responsibility. Not even pretending to be a trained historian, I have relied instead on curiosity and enthusiasm for the past to provide, I hope, a glimpse of what our forebears did, thought, said and wrote in and near the delightful Hamford Water.

P.C.F.

BIBLIOGRAPHY

Irene Johnson	Turning point
Ernest A Wood	A history of Thorpe-le-Soken to the year 1890
Hervey Benham	Codbangers
Gladys A Ward	Victorian and Edwardian Brentwood
Kenneth J Neale	Essex in history
J F C Harrison	The common people
John Gooders	Birds that came back
Glyn Morgan	Secret Essex
C V Smith	Cockney boy in Essex
Hilda Grieve	The great tide
Gurney Benham	Essex Sokens
David Thompson	England in the Nineteenth Century
G M Trevelyan	Illustrated English social history
J Uglow	Sailorman: a bargemaster's story
Richard H Perks	Sprits'l
Arthur Freeling	Flowers, their use and beauty in language and sentiment
Clifford Bax	Highways and byways in Essex
A F J Brown	Essex people, 1750-1900
Stanley Jermyn	Flora of Essex
Clare Lloyd	Birdwatching on estuaries, coast and sea
Derek Roe	Prehistory
John Burnett	Useful toil: autobiographies of working people from 1820 to 1920
J M Stratton	Agricultural records, AD 220-1977
Hervey Benham	The smugglers' century
F J Speakman	A poacher's tale
M StJ Parker & D J Reid	The British revolution, 1750-1970
Victoria History of Essex, Vol. 2, 1907	
J Wentworth Day	Essex and Suffolk pubs
V T J Arkell	Britain transformed
Townsend Warner	Landmarks in English industrial history
Thomas B Peacock	The Mistley, Thorpe & Walton Railway
K S Inglis	Churches and the working classes in Victorian England
S C Carpenter	Church and people, 1789-1889
Peter Salway	Roman Britain
David Corke	The nature of Essex

GENERAL INDEX

BIOGRAPHICAL INDEX

TOPOGRAPHICAL INDEX

Note: Hamford Water, Kirby-le-Soken, Kirby Quay, Beaumont Quay and Landermere Quay appear too frequently for indexing